NEW

Total English

Pearson Education Limited
Edinburgh Gate
Harlow
Essex CM20 2JE
England
and Associated Companies throughout the world.

www.pearsonELT.com

First published 2012

ISBN 978-1-4082-5462-2
Book with Active Book Pack

Set in MetaPlusBook-Roman
Printed in Slovakia by Neografia

Acknowledgements

The publishers and author would like to thank the following people and institutions for their feedback and comments during the development of the material:
Witoslaw Awedyk, Adam Mickiewicz University, Logistics College in Poznan, Poland; Nigel Barnsley, Spain; Nathaniel Barrett, EC London, UK; Alvaro Catañeda, Instituto de Lenguas de la Universidad Distrital, Columbia; Victor Cinti, ECC Osaka, Japan; David Corp, Merit UPC, Spain; Alper Darici, Fatih High School, Turkey; Laura L'Eglise, France; Lech Krzeminski, Maria Curie-Sklodowska University in Lublin, Poland; Adriana Lima, ELT Academic Consultant, Brazil; Bojana Le Pocreau, CCI Maine-et-Loire, France; Eszter Timár, Central European University, Hungary; Tom Windle, Japan.

We are grateful to the following for permission to reproduce copyright material:

Logos
Logo 5.1 from Twitter logo and screenshot, copyright © 2011, Twitter.

Photo acknowledgements

The publisher would like to thank the following for their kind permission to reproduce their photographs:

(Key: b-bottom; c-centre; l-left; r-right; t-top)

Alamy Images: 16cl (B), 124tr, alam 32 (C), Alex Segre 39tl (B), Anyka 90br (8), blickwinkel 39t (A), Bruce McGowan 32 (G), Caro 83bl/1, Greg Balfour Evans 106cr (B), Hemis 9tl (B), Hugh Threlfall 22 (L), 115bl, JoeFox 65 (F), Juice Images 90br (5), Michael Kemp 29cl (C), Niels Poulsen simi3 122tc, Ozimages 103br, Pascal Saez 120cl (2), Peter Titmuss 106tr (A), PhotoSlinger 32 (E), Purepix 100bc, Rob Wilkinson 52b (B), Robert Read Road Signs 32 (F), Ronald Greer 56br, Shoosmith Railway Collection 45tl, studiomode 23c, 115tl, VStock 90cr (1); **Caters News Agency:** 93cr/1, 93cr/3, 118bl, 118br; **Corbis:** AID / amanaimages 22t, Ariel Skelley / Blend Images 90cr/6, Beau Lark 14bl, Bettmann 127tr, Chris Carroll 106br (D), cultura 89cl (B), Dave & Les Jacobs / cultura 73cr, Frank Rothe 93cr/2, 114b, Henglein and Steets / cultura 10tr (2), Jerry Cooke 79t (A), Jose Luis Pelaez, Inc. / Blend Images 64t, Kevin Dodge 112tc, 117, Kim Kulish 79bl (D), Luca Tettoni 59bl (D), Martin Sundberg 99bl (C), Patrick Lane / Blend Images 14tl, Raygun / cultura 65cl, Ron Nickel / Design Pics 94tc, Vivek Prakash / Reuters 72br; **Fotolia.com:** alekc79 22/top of 2 (O), Alexirius 22 (C), amlet 22 (J), 115tr, Arkhipov 22 (M), Arsentyeva E 22 (N), Bartek Magierowski 123tl, Borodaev 22 (G), shapovalova 115tc/2, chas53 22 (I), diego cervo 102tr (5), Edyta Pawlowska 19t, Jessica Bethke 101br, Joe Gough 31 (10), karaboux 51 (5), Kondor83 51 (2), Kwest 50t, Liliia Rudchenko 31 (8), shapovalova 22 (B), Marc Dietrich 115c/2, Marcin Sadlowski

103cl (9), markrhiggins 22 (D), martinlee 31 (4), Miroslav 102tl/1, mlehmann78 40cl, montica 51 (6), Oleg Ivanov 115bl/2, Oleksiy Ilyashenko 31 (1), Olga Khopshanosova 22 (A), Pippa West 82cl (4), robynmac 23t, RTimages 22 (E), Sashkin 65 (E), Simone van den Berg 54c, Tim 22 (H), Vladimir Pogorelov 31 (5); **Getty Images:** A.B. 56cr, Alain Daussin 54b, altrendo images 63tl, altrendo images 19bl (D), 20cr, Amy Eckert 69cl (C), Barry Yee 24tl (1), Britt Erlanson 112tr, 117br, Bruce Laurance 24tr (2), Burke / Triolo Productions 112br, 117tr, Caroline Purser 39bl (D), Dan Kitwood 49t, Diamond Images 80c (8), Erik Dreyer 90cr (3), Gamma-Keystone 80c (2), Getty Images 12cl (2), 12bl (3), 13tl (1), Getty Images 80c (1), 80c (11), 80c (4), 80c (5), 80c (6), 80c (7), 80c (9), 81cl, 109t, Getty Images Entertainment 12t, Henry Wolf 83bl, Jaime Kowal 19cl (C), James Cotier 49cl (C), Jason Todd 99bl (D), Jed Share 72br/2, John-Francis Bourke 69t (A), joSon 62b, Jupiter images 24t, 24tr, LWA 99cl (B), Marc Romanelli 22b, Marcus Mok 26bl, Nick Daly 82cl (1), Nisian Hughes 36t, Patrick Dieudonne 39cl (C), Pinnacle Pictures 20tr, Redferns 80c (10), 80c (3), Robert Daly 49bl (D), Robert Llewellyn 125tc, Ron Krisel 18br, Sean Murphy 126bl, Susan Seubert 32tr (B), Tim Robberts 69tl (B), Tom Grill 104tc, WIN-Initiative 49tl (B), WireImage 21cl, 21br, WireImage 116cl, 116b, Yellow Dog Productions 10tl (1), Zubin Shroff 104cr; **Ronald Grant Archive:** 14t, Canal 14br, RKO RADIO PICTURES 15b; **iStockphoto:** bradwieland 32tl (A), pastorscott 32c (D); **Kevin Richardson:** 72cr; **Kobal Collection Ltd:** Alta Vista 14b, Warner Bros 14tr; **Lonely Planet Images:** John Maier Jr 54bl, Phil Weymouth 30tr (B), Richard I'Anson 9t (A), Tony Wheeler 89t (A); **Masterfile UK Ltd:** Peter Griffith 89cl (C); **Pearson Education Ltd:** 22 (P), 22tr (2nd cover); **Photolibrary.com:** 65 (B), Asia Images Group 52br (C), B Boissonnet 29bl (D), bilderlounge 10cr (3), Brigitte Sporrer (C), Cedric Cedric 52tr, Corbis 89bl (D), Corbis InsideOut Pix 59t (A), Creasource 121tr, Daniel Grill 9cl (C), Daniel Bosworth 69bl (D), David Jerome Ball 117tl, David Wall 106cr (C), DEA C SAPPA 123tr, Drive Images 90bl (4), eVox Productions LLC 120cr (4), Fiona Jackson-Downes 52bl (A), fotog 60-61t, Fresh Food Images 30cl (A), Grant Pritchard 29t, imagebroker rf 31 (3), Imagesource 16tl (A), Juice Images 121cr, Kablonk! 20br, Paddy Eckersley 86tr, Radius Images 59tl (B), Ray Laskowitz 30br (C), Ron Nickel 59cl (C), Stockbrokerxtra Images 88bl, Tim Pannell /
Corbis 50tl, Tom Merton 9bl (D), Tony Latham 44t, Travel Pix 45br; **Plainpicture Ltd:** Johner 19tl (B); **Press Association Images:** Tommy Schonstedt / XP / Scanpix 92tr; **Rex Features:** Agencia EFE 13cr (4), 112c/4, Courtesy Everett Collection 79cl (C), David Hartley 21cr, 116t, Garo / Phanie 90bl (7), Geoff Moore 21bl, 116c, Image Source 29tl (B), Isifa Image Service sro 13cl (3), 109c/3, Nick White / Mood Board 99tr (A), Rex Features 12tl (1), 13tr (2), 79cl (B), 112tl/2, Sipa Press 13br (6), 112b/6, Theo Kingma 13bl (5), 109b/5, Tim Rooke 21tl, 21tr, 116tc, 116cr; **Shutterstock.com:** Alexei Nikolaevich 22/ bottom of 2 (O), Anetta 83cr/2, Arieliona 103tc (3), AVAVA 50cr, beerkoff 82cl (2), Blend Images 82cl (3), Cheryl Casey 103tl (8), claires 22 (F), 115bc/1, Cloudia Newland 100tr, Damir Huskic 100cl (A), Elena Elisseeva 90cl (2), Ilja Mašík 65 (H), ILYA GENKIN 31 (7), Kirsty Pargeter 114c, kkymek 65 (G), lculig 31 (9), Liviu Toader 119cr, Lucian Coman 61tc (chris), LVV 105br, maggee 22 (K), Maksym Bondarchuk 23b, Mariusz Gwizdon 65 (C), Maugli 51 (4), Michelangelo Gratton 62tr, MishAl 65 (A), Nayashkova Olga 120tr (3), ostill 128cl, Pavel Pustina 112bc, 117 (claire), Photobank 103tl (7), Photocrea 65 (D), PhotoHouse 115cl/2, Poulsons Photography 102tr (6), Sergey Peterman 31 (6), taelove7 115c/1, 115cl/1, travis manley 122tl, Valentyn Volkov 115tl/2, Valua Vitaly 112bl, 117t, 120tl, vblinov 122tr, Viktor1 31 (2), Yuri Arcurs 103tl (2), 112, 117bl, Yuri Arcurs 61c (fiona), Zurijeta 103tr (4); **'South Bank, Bankside and London Bridge InfoBikes, photography by Libera PR' www.southbanklondon.com** 42tr; **Splash News:** Angel Chevrestt 61tl

Cover images: *Front* **Photolibrary.com:** Hill Creek Pictures BV

All other images © Pearson Education

Every effort has been made to trace the copyright holders and we apologise in advance for any unintentional omissions. We would be pleased to insert the appropriate acknowledgement in any subsequent edition of this publication.

Illustrated by Ilias Arahovitis, Norbert Sipos (both from Beehive Illustrations), Joanne Kerr (New Division), Ian Mitchell (Three in a box), Roarr Design.

NEW

Total English

STARTER

Students' Book

Jonathan Bygrave

Contents

Contents

Contents

Contents

Classroom language

1 🔘 1.01 Listen and repeat the words.

1 read

2 write

3 speak

4 listen

5 match

6 repeat

7 look

8 choose

9 complete

2 🔘 1.02 Listen and repeat the useful phrases.

1 Can you repeat that, please?
2 What's *Hola* in English?
3 Sorry, I don't understand.
4 What does *complete* mean?
5 Can you help me, please?
6 What's the answer to number 4?

Lead-in

1 **a** Look at the words in the box. Tick (✓) the words you know.

> bank ☐   bus ☐   café ☐   chocolate ☐
> cinema ☐   coffee ☐   computer ☐   doctor ☐
> film ☐   football ☐   hotel ☐   Internet ☐
> passport ☐   pizza ☐   police ☐   restaurant ☐
> salad ☐   student ☐   taxi ☐   telephone ☐
> television ☐   university ☐

b 🔊 1.03 Listen and repeat the words.

2 Work in pairs and look at the photos. What can you see?

A: *a bus*

3 What other English words do you know? Add words to the table.

Places	Food	Sport	Other
theatre	spaghetti	tennis	piano

1.1 Nice to meet you!

A: Hi. I'm Kate. What's your name?
B: My name's Clive.
A: Nice to meet you.
B: Nice to meet you, too.

A: Hello, Mr Smith. I'm Doctor Mazur.
B: Hello. Nice to meet you.
A: Nice to meet you, too.

A: Hello.
B: Hello. My name's Iris Salas.
A: Welcome to Hotel Panorama, Ms Salas.
B: Thank you.
A: You're in room 3–1–5.

Speaking

1 a 🔊 1.04 Read and listen to the dialogues.

b Listen again and repeat the dialogues.

2 In pairs, practise the dialogues.
A: *Hi. I'm Kate. What's your name?*
B: *My name's Clive.*

3 Say your name in English.
I'm Maria.   *My name's Stefan.*

Pronunciation | /aɪ/

4 a 🔊 1.05 Listen and repeat the words.
/aɪ/ Hi I Clive Iris nice my

b 🔊 1.06 Listen and repeat the sentences.
1 Hi, I'm Clive.
2 Hi Clive. My name's Iris.
3 Nice to meet you.
4 Nice to meet you, too.

Grammar | *to be: I and you*

5 Read the sentences. Write the words in **bold** in the Active grammar box.

1 **You're** in room 3–1–5.　　2 **I'm** Clive.

Active grammar

_____ = *I am*　　_____ = *you are*

---

see Reference page 17

6 **a** Choose the correct words in *italics*.

1 **A:** Hello. *I'm*/*You're* Doctor Rolf.
　B: Hello, Doctor Rolf. *I'm*/*You're* Jane.
2 **A:** Welcome to Hotel Central.
　B: Thank you. *I'm*/*You're* Mr Smith.
　A: *I'm*/*You're* in room 2–9–6, Mr Smith.

b Complete the dialogues with *I'm* or *you're*.

1 **A:** Hello. _____ Dino. What's your name?
　B: _____ Rosa.

2 **A:** Welcome to Hotel Europa. What's your name?
　B: _____ Edward Presley.
　A: _____ in room 6–2–8, Mr Presley.
　B: Thank you.

Vocabulary | numbers 0–10

7 **a** 🌐 1.07 Listen and repeat the numbers 0–10.

0	**zero/oh**
1	**one**
2	**two**
3	**three**
4	**four**
5	**five**
6	**six**
7	**seven**
8	**eight**
9	**nine**
10	**ten**

b Work in pairs.
Student A: say two numbers.
Student B: say the next number.
A: *seven, eight ...*
B: *nine*

Speaking

8 🌐 1.08 Listen and respond.

1 Nice to meet you.
　Nice to meet you, too.
2 Hello. I'm Paul Smith.
3 Welcome to Hotel Panorama.
4 Hi. What's your name?

9 Say hello to other students in the class.

A: *Hello.*
B: *Hi.*
A: *I'm Maria. What's your name?*
B: *My name's Stefan.*
A: *Nice to meet you.*
B: *Nice to meet you, too.*

Fashion quiz
the faces behind the names

1 Who's he?
   a Calvin Klein   **b** Giorgio Armani

   Where is he from?
   a Spain   **b** Italy

2 Who's she?
   a Donna Karan   **b** Donatella Versace

   Where is she from?
   a The USA   **b** The UK

3 Who's he?
   a Jimmy Choo   **b** Issey Miyake

   Where is he from?
   a China   **b** Malaysia

Score = ___ / 6

Listening

1 Work in pairs. Do the fashion quiz.

2 **a** 🔊 1.09 Listen to Mike and Nora and check your answers. What is your score?

   b Listen again. What is Nora's score?

Vocabulary | countries

3 **a** 🔊 1.10 Listen and repeat the countries.

	Argentina			Japan
	Brazil			Mexico
	China			Poland
	France			Russia
	Germany			Spain
	India			the UK
	Italy			the USA

b Work in pairs.
Student A: cover the country word and point to a flag.
Student B: say the country.

4 **a** 🔊 1.11 Listen and complete the How to... box.

> ### How to... ask where someone is from
> ---
> A: *Where are you from, Becky?*
> B: *I'm from* (1) _____ .
> A: *Where in* (2) _____ .
> B: (3) _____ .

b Listen again and repeat the dialogue.

5 Ask and answer with other students.
   A: *Where are you from, Karol?*
   B: *I'm from Hungary.*
   A: *Where in Hungary?*
   B: *Budapest.*

Grammar | *to be*: *he, she* and *it*

6 **a** Read part of the dialogue from exercise 2 and underline *'s*, *is* and *isn't*.

Mike: Question two. Who's she?

Nora: Is she Donatella Versace?

Mike: No, she isn't. She's Donna Karan. And where is Donna Karan from?

Nora: Well, she isn't from the UK so ... she's from the USA.

Mike: Correct!

b Complete the Active grammar box with *is* or *isn't*.

Active grammar

➕ | *He's/She's/It's from Italy.*

➖ | *He/She/It _____ from the USA.*

❓ | *_____ he/she/it from China?*

Yes, he/she/it _____ .
No, he/she/it _____ .

Who's he/she?
Where is (Where's) he/she/it from?

---

see Reference page 17

7 Choose the correct answers.

1 **A:** Is she from Spain?
  B: Yes, _____ .
  a she   **b** she's   **c** she is

2 **A:** Who's he?
  B: _____ Calvin Klein.
  a He   **b** He's   **c** Is he

3 **A:** Is he Giorgio Armani?
  B: No, _____ .
  a he   **b** he is no   **c** he isn't

4 _____ she from?
  a Where   **b** Where's   **c** Is where

5 **A:** _____ a quiz?
  a Is   **b** Is it   **c** It is
  B: Yes, _____ .
  a is   **b** it's   **c** it is

6 _____ your name?
  a What   **b** Is what   **c** What's

8 Work in pairs. Ask about other students in your class.

A: *Who's she?*
B: *She's Ivana.*
A: *Where's she from?*

Pronunciation | contractions

9 **a** 🔵 1.12 Listen and repeat the contractions.

I'm you're he's she's it's isn't who's where's

b 🔵 1.13 Listen and repeat the sentences.

1 I'm from Spain and she's from China.
2 It isn't a film quiz. It's a fashion quiz.
3 Who's he? He isn't a student.
4 She's from Germany and she's in room three.
5 Where's she from? Is she from Poland?

Speaking

10 **a** Work in pairs. Ask and answer *Who's he/she?* and *Where's he/she from?*

b Check your answers.
Student A: look at page 109.
Student B: look at page 112.

13

Reading

1 Work in pairs. What's your favourite film?

My favourite film is ...

2 **a** Read about Ashna, Simon, Flavia and Hiro. Match the film posters with the people.

Ashna = Sholay

What's your favourite film?

Ashna: My favourite film is *Sholay*. It's an Indian film and I'm Indian, too. Simon's British. His favourite film is *Inception*. It's American. I'm Bollywood and he's Hollywood!

What's your favourite film?

Hiro: Flavia's Brazilian and her favourite film is Brazilian, too. It's *Central Station*. I'm Japanese but my favourite film is Mexican. It's *Amores Perros*.

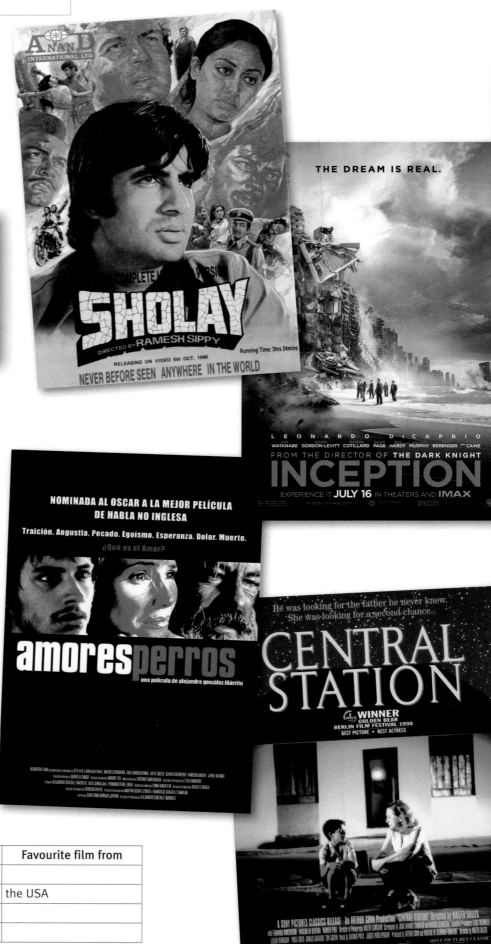

b Read again and complete the table.

	From	Favourite film from
Ashna	India	
Simon		the USA
Hiro		
Flavia		

14

Vocabulary | nationalities

3 Complete the table.

Country	Nationality	Ending
Bra<u>zil</u>	(1) *Brazilian*	*(i)an*
<u>Ger</u>many	German	
<u>In</u>dia	(2) _____	
<u>It</u>aly	Italian	
<u>Mex</u>ico	(3) _____	
<u>Rus</u>sia	Russian	
the USA	(4) _____	
<u>Po</u>land	<u>Po</u>lish	*ish*
Spain	(5) _____	
the UK	<u>Bri</u>tish	
<u>Chi</u>na	Chi<u>nese</u>	*ese*
<u>Ja</u>pan	(6) _____	

Pronunciation | syllable stress

4 **a** 🌐 1.14 Listen and repeat the countries and nationality words.

b Listen again. How many syllables are in each word? Why are some syllables <u>underlined</u>?

It–a–ly = 3 syllables
I–<u>tal</u>–i–an = 4 syllables

5 Work in pairs. Say a country. Your partner says the nationality. Practise the stress.

A: *India* B: *Indian*

6 Look at the Lifelong learning box. Read the tip.

A vocabulary notebook

❗ Write new words in a vocabulary notebook. Show the stress.

Countries	Nationalities
Mexico	*Mexican*
Germany	*German*

Lifelong learning

Grammar | possessive adjectives: *my*, *your*, *his* and *her*

7 Read the sentences. Complete the Active grammar box with the words in **bold**.

1 **His** favourite film is *Pulp Fiction*.
2 What's **your** favourite film?
3 **Her** favourite film is Brazilian.

Active grammar

I	*my*	he	_____
you	_____	she	_____

see Reference page 17

8 Choose the correct words in *italics*.

1 *He's/His* Rafael. *He's/His* favourite food is pizza.
2 *She's/Her* name is Lisa. *She's/Her* favourite film is *Red*.
3 What's *you/your* name? Where are *you/your* from?
4 *I/My* name's Sven. *I/My* favourite sport is football.

9 Complete the interview with *my*, *your*, *his* or *her*.

Interviewer: What's (1) _____ name?
Kate: (2) _____ name's Kate.
Interviewer: Who's he?
Kate: (3) _____ name's Tom. He's six.
Interviewer: What's (4) _____ favourite film?
Kate: It's *Toy Story*. And (5) _____ favourite actor is Brad Pitt.
Interviewer: What's Kate's favourite film, Tom?
Tom: (6) _____ favourite film is *P.S. I Love You*. Yuk!

Speaking

10 **a** Look at page 116 and do the survey for you.

b Work in groups of three. Ask and answer the questions and complete the survey.

A: *What's your favourite film?*
B: *It's* La Dolce Vita.
A: *Is that Italian?*
B: *Yes, it is.*

c Tell the class about one person in your group.

Marco's favourite film is It's a Wonderful Life. *It's an American film. His favourite food is ...*

1 | Communication

1 **a** 🔊 1.15 Listen and repeat the phone numbers.

1 729 1553
2 07863 400212
3 01873 839711

b How do we say these numbers? Listen again and check.

0 = '_____'   55 = '_____ _____'

2 🔊 1.16 Listen and correct these numbers.

1 My mobile number is 0583 121 668.
2 My home number is 932 81009.
3 My work number is 01872 698470.

3 **a** 🔊 1.17 Listen. Match the dialogues (1–3) with the photos (A–C).

Dialogue 1 = photo ___C___
Dialogue 2 = photo _____
Dialogue 3 = photo _____

b Listen again and write the phone numbers.

Dialogue 1: 0747 _ _ _ _ _ _
Dialogue 2: 0208 _ _ _ _ _ _ _
Dialogue 3: 0118 _ _ _ _ _ _ _

4 **a** 🔊 1.18 Complete the How to... box. Then listen and check.

> ## How to... ask for repetition
>
> A: *What's your mobile number?*
> B: *It's 0749 128384.*
> A: *Sorry. Can you (1) _____ that again?*
> B: *Yes, it's 0749 128384. And my work number is 01532 229150.*
> A: *Sorry. Could you (2) _____ that?*
> B: *Yes, it's 01532 229150.*
> A: *Thanks.*

b Work in pairs. Practise the dialogue in the How to... box.

5 Work in groups of three. Exchange information about Leonardo, Sofia and Marta and complete the table.

Student A: look at page 118.   **Student C:** look at page 116.
Student B: look at page 114.

	Leonardo	Sofia	Marta
From (country)	*Mexico*		
From (city)			
Mobile phone number			
Home number			

A: *Where is Leonardo from?*
B: *He's from Mexico.*
A: *Where in Mexico?*

to be: *I, you, he, she* and *it*

⊕   *I'm* Kate. *(am)*
     You're in room 3. *(are)*
     He's from Spain. *(is)*
     She's Italian. *(is)*
     It's a pizza. *(is)*

⊖   *I'm not* American. *(am not)*
     You **aren't** a student./You**'re not** a student. *(are not)*
     He **isn't** from the UK./He**'s not** from the UK.
     She **isn't** Indian./She**'s not** Indian. *(is not)*
     It **isn't** from China./It**'s not** from China.

❓		
Am I late?	Yes, you are./No, you aren't.
Are you British?	Yes, I am./No, I'm not.
Is he from France?	Yes, he is./No, he isn't.
Is she Emma?	Yes, she is./No, she isn't.
Is it a bank?	Yes, it is./No, it isn't.

I am, he is, is not, etc are **full forms**.
I'm, he's, isn't, etc are **contractions**.
We use contractions when we speak and often when we write.

! Remember!
A: *Are you from Mexico?*
B: *Yes, I am.* ~~Yes, I'm.~~

Wh- questions

What
A: *What's your name?*
B: *My name's Svetlana.*

A: *What's your mobile number?*
B: *It's 07833 383 211.*

A: *What's your favourite film?*
B: *It's Avatar.*

Where
A: *Where are you from?*
B: *I'm from Poland.*

A: *Where in Poland?*
B: *Katowice.*

Who
A: *Who's he?*
B: *He's Giorgio Armani.*

Possessive adjectives: *my, your, his* and *her*

Pronouns	Possessive adjectives
I'm Robert.	**My** favourite film is The Matrix.
You're Mina.	**Your** favourite actor is Johnny Depp.
He's Yuri.	**His** favourite city is Moscow.
She's Cristina.	**Her** number is 0114 384 339.
It's a computer.	**Its** hard disk is 500GB.

Key vocabulary

International words

bank   bus   café   chocolate   cinema   coffee   computer   doctor   film   football   hotel   Internet   passport   pizza   police   restaurant   salad   student   taxi   telephone   television   university

Numbers 0–10

0	zero ('oh' in telephone numbers)
1	one
2	two
3	three
4	four
5	five
6	six
7	seven
8	eight
9	nine
10	ten

Countries and nationalities

Country	Nationality
Argentina	Argentinian
Brazil	Brazilian
China	Chinese
France	French
Germany	German
India	Indian
Italy	Italian
Japan	Japanese
Mexico	Mexican
Poland	Polish
Russia	Russian
Spain	Spanish
the UK	British
the USA	American

Listen to the explanations and vocabulary.
ACTIVEBOOK

see Writing bank page 120

1 Review and practice

1 Put the words in the correct order to make sentences.

1 A: your name? What's

What's your name?

B: name's My Rick.

A: meet Rick. you, Nice to

2 A: Hotel Lux. to Welcome

B: Thank you. name's Hardy. Mr My

A: room You're 4–1–7, in Mr Hardy.

2 Complete the sentences with *he, she* or *it* and the correct form of *to be*.

1 Sushi: *It isn't* from Germany. *It's from* Japan.

2 Queen Elizabeth: *Is she* British? Yes, she is.

3 Madonna: _____ Italian. _____ American.

4 Lionel Messi: _____ Brazilian? No, _____ . _____ from Argentina.

5 Sony: _____ Chinese. _____ Japanese.

6 Champagne: _____ from France? Yes, _____ .

7 Vladimir Putin: _____ Polish. _____ Russian.

8 Adidas: _____ American? No, _____ . _____ German.

3 Rewrite the sentences with contractions.

1 You are a student.

You're a student.

2 She is not German.

3 What is his name?

4 I am not Lee. I am Leo.

5 Who is she?

6 It is not a café. It is a restaurant.

7 Where is he from? Is he American?

8 You are not Italian. You are French.

4 Complete the dialogue with *my, your, his* or *her*.

5 **a** Complete the dialogue with *he, he's* or *his*.

A: What's (1) *his* name?

B: (2) _____ name's Martin.

A: Where's (3) _____ from?

B: (4) _____ from the UK.

A: Is (5) _____ from London?

B: No, he isn't. (6) _____ from Manchester.

b Complete the dialogue with *she, she's* or *her*.

A: Who's (1) _____ ?

B: (2) _____ Maria.

A: Where's (3) _____ from?

B: (4) _____ from Spain.

A: What's (5) _____ favourite film?

B: I don't know!

6 Match the words to the stress patterns.

café cinema computer doctor football
Internet passport police salad telephone

1 Oo   *café* _____ _____ _____ _____

2 oO   _____

3 Ooo   _____ _____ _____

4 oOo   _____

7 Rewrite the sentences with nationalities.

1 My favourite food is from China.

My favourite food is Chinese.

2 Is she from Spain?

3 My car isn't from Germany.

4 My favourite music is from the UK.

5 Is Al Pacino from the USA?

6 Is Lady Gaga from Poland?

7 Is his television from Japan?

8 My favourite films are from Mexico.

Interviewer: What's (1) *your* name?

Dan: (2) _____ name's Dan.

Interviewer: And what's (3) _____ name?

Dan: (4) _____ name's Pip. She's seven.

Interviewer: What's (5) _____ favourite food?

Dan: I don't know. What's (6) _____ favourite food, Pip?

Pip: It's pizza.

Interviewer: Pip, what's (7) _____ favourite food?

Pip: (8) _____ favourite food is pizza too.

Dan: No, it isn't! (9) _____ favourite food is salad.

Pip

Dan

Kim

A

Lead-in

B

1 **a** Look at the words in the box. Tick (✓) the words you know.

> aunt ☐   boyfriend ☐   brother ☐   cousin ☐
> daughter ☐   father (dad) ☐   friend ☐   girlfriend ☐
> grandfather (grandpa) ☐   grandmother (grandma) ☐
> husband ☐   mother (mum) ☐   sister ☐   son ☐
> uncle ☐   wife ☐

b 🔵 1.19 Listen and repeat the words.

2 Match the dialogues with the photos.

Ann: Who's she?
Kim: She's my sister. She's with my mother and my grandmother. ☐

Ann: Who's he?
Kim: He's Uncle Henry. She's Aunt Paula and she's my cousin, Tara. ☐

Ann: Is he your husband?
Kim: Yes, he is. And she's my daughter, Tara. And she's my other daughter, Lily. ☐

Ann: Is he your uncle?
Kim: No, he isn't. He's my father. He's with my brother, Jon, and his son, Callum. ☐

C

D

3 Complete the table with the words in exercise 1.

Male ♂	Female ♀	Male or female
brother	*sister*	*cousin*

4 Work in pairs. Write the names of five people in your family. Ask and answer questions about the names.
A: *Who's Kerem?*   **B:** *He's my brother.*

19

2.1 Family parties

Grammar	*to be*: *you* (plural), *we* and *they*; possessive adjectives: *our*, *your* and *their*
Can do	introduce a friend

Vocabulary | the alphabet

1 **a** Can you say the vowels in English?

a e i o u

b 🔊 1.20 Listen and check. Then listen again and repeat the sounds.

2 **a** 🔊 1.21 Say the whole alphabet in English. Then listen and check.

a b c d e f g h i j k l m
n o p q r s t u v w x y z

b Listen again and repeat the sounds.

c Look at the alphabet again. Say the letters of the same colour. What sound do they have in common?

a, h, j, k

3 **a** 🔊 1.22 Listen to the dialogue.

A: What's your name?
B: Billy.
A: How do you spell that?
B: B–I–double L–Y.

b Work in pairs. Practise the dialogue with your names.

Listening

4 **a** 🔊 1.23 Listen and complete dialogues 1–3 on the right with family words.

b Listen again and read. Answer the questions.

1 Is Hiro late?
2 What is Hiro's full name?
3 Where are Grandma and Grandpa?
4 What is Baby Boris?
5 Are Helen and Liz cousins?
6 Are Helen and Alfie married?

5 **a** Work in groups of three. Practise the dialogue in the How to... box.

> ### How to... introduce someone
>
> **A:** *Erica, this is James.*
> **B:** *Nice to meet you, James.*
> **C:** *Nice/Good to meet you too, Erica.*

b Introduce each other.

Dialogue 1
A: Hi (1) _____ . Are we late?
B: No, you aren't. Come in, Hiro.
A: Mum, Dad, this is Alice, my new (2) _____ .
B: Nice to meet you, Alice.
C: Nice to meet you, too, Mrs Tanaka.

Dialogue 2
A: Are (3) _____ here?
B: Yes, they are. They're outside with Baby Boris.
A: Baby Boris? Who's Baby Boris?
B: Not who – what. It's their new sports car.

Dialogue 3
A: This is Alfie. He's Helen's new boyfriend.
B: Hello Alfie. I'm Liz and this is my sister, Mina. Nice to meet you.
C: Nice to meet you, too. Is Helen your (4) _____ ?
B: No, she isn't. She's our (5) _____ .

Grammar 1 | *to be: you* (plural) *we* and *they*

6 **a** Read the dialogues in exercise 4a again. <u>Underline</u> the examples of *'re*, *are* and *aren't*.

b Complete the Active grammar box with *are* or *aren't*.

> ### Active grammar
>
> ➕ *You're/We're/They're late. (are)*
>
> ➖ *You/We/They _____ married. (are not)*
>
> ❓ *_____ you/we/they outside?*
>
> *Yes, you/we/they _____ .*
>
> *No, you/we/they _____ .*

see Reference page 27

7 **a** Write sentences and questions with *you, we* or *they* and *to be*.

1 Eduardo and I/brother and sister

We're brother and sister.

2 You and Claudia/married? // Yes

Are you married? Yes, we are.

3 Aunt Petra and Uncle Paul/in the garden? // No

4 You and I/not late

5 Giang and Lam/not Chinese

6 Adam and I/from Poland

7 Lucy and you/late? // No

8 Roman and I/from Moscow

9 Mr and Mrs Swinton/in love

b 🔵 1.24 Listen and check your answers. Then repeat the sentences.

Grammar 2 | possessive adjectives: *our, your* and *their*

8 Complete the sentences from the dialogues in exercise 4a with *our, your* or *their*.

> ### Active grammar
>
> *She's _____ cousin.*
>
> *Is she _____ friend?*
>
> *It's _____ sports car.*

see Reference page 27

9 **a** Complete the dialogues with *our, your* or *their*.

1 **Peter:** How do you spell _____ names?

 Ian: I'm Ian, I–A–N, and she's Ruth, R–U–T–H.

2 **Adam:** I'm Adam and this is my brother, Ben.

 Ben: And this is _____ mother, Barbara.

3 **Carol:** Lisa and Fran are sisters.

 Bob: Is Alan _____ father?

 Carol: No, he isn't. He's _____ uncle.

4 **Andy:** Hi, Olga. Hi, Natalia. Where are _____ passports?

 Olga: They're in my bag.

b 🔵 1.25 Listen and check your answers. Then repeat the dialogues.

Speaking

10 Work in pairs.

Student A: ask Student B questions about the family in the photographs. Ask about names and family relations.

Student B: look at page 116. Answer Student A's questions.

A: *Who are they?*

B: *They're Prince William and Prince Harry.*

A: *And who's she?*

B: *She's Sophie.*

A: *Is she their mother?*

B: *No, she isn't. She's their aunt.*

2.2 What's in your bag?

Grammar *a/an*, noun plurals

Can do list the contents of your bag

Vocabulary | personal objects

1 **a** 🔊 1.26 Listen and repeat the words.

apple ☑	book ☐	brush ☐
business card ☐	camera ☐	
comp<u>u</u>ter ☐	iPod ☐	key ☐
<u>mo</u>bile (phone) ☐	orange ☐	
passport ☐	pen ☐	purse ☐
(train) ticket ☐	umbr<u>e</u>lla ☐	
watch ☐		

b Match the words in the box with the photos.

2 Work in pairs.

Student A: say a letter, A–P.

Student B: say the object.

Pronunciation | /æ/ and /e/

3 **a** 🔊 1.27 Listen and repeat the words.

/æ/ apple camera grandpa café bag

/e/ pen Internet umbrella friend seven

b <u>Underline</u> the /æ/ sounds and ⟨circle⟩ the /e/ sounds in the sentences.

1 My camera and my umbrella are in my bag.

2 I'm in a taxi and my friend is in a café.

3 What's in my bag? Ten pens and an apple.

c 🔊 1.28 Listen and check your answers. Then repeat the sentences.

4 Look at the Lifelong learning box. Read the tip.

English sounds

❗ Learn how to say two English sounds every week. Use them in your vocabulary notebook.

/æ/
c<u>a</u>mera *My camera is in my bag.*

/e/
fri<u>e</u>nd *She's my best friend.*

Lifelong learning

Lilly

Jeff

22

Grammar | *a/an*; noun plurals

5 **a** Read the texts. Find five differences between the texts and the photos.

LILLY: 66 Hi. I'm Lilly. I'm half Chinese, half British. What's in my bag? Well, a computer and a mobile phone, of course. And two passports – my Chinese passport and my British passport. And my keys, two brushes, my purse, an umbrella and … and a business card. 99

JEFF: 66 Hello. I'm Jeff. I'm American. What's in my bag? Er … an apple, two oranges, an iPod for my music … and a book – *Catch 22* by Joseph Heller. It's a great book. What else? Er … a camera, two pens, two watches … oh, and a train ticket to Paris. 99

b Read the text again and complete the Active grammar box.

Active grammar

a/an

a	book	_____	apple
	camera		iPod

Noun plurals

1 Regular

one pen | two pen___
one passport | two passport___

2 Nouns ending in *-s*, *-sh*, or *-ch*

one brush | two brush___
one watch | two watch___

---

see Reference page 27

6 🔊 1.29 Listen to the text in exercise 5a. How is 'a' pronounced?

7 **a** Label the pictures.

①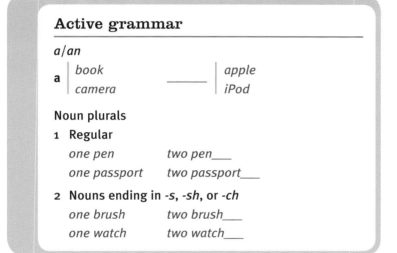

a mobile phone

② two business cards

③ _____

④ _____

⑤ _____

⑥ _____

⑦ _____

⑧ _____

⑨ _____

b 🔊 1.30 Listen and check your answers. Then repeat the words.

---

8 Read the text and find four more mistakes.

File Edit View Go Bookmarks Tools Help

http://www.ebidder.co.uk/

ebidder.co.uk

For sale: various objects
Condition: used
Quantity: 1
Price: £10.00
Bids: 4   **Bid now**

What is for sale?

A
• ╳ German watch
It's from Berlin and it's great watch.

• Two mobile phone
They are Chinese phone.

• My computer
It's Japanese computer.

Done

Speaking

9 Work in pairs. Turn to page 115. Look at the photos for one minute. Then close your books and try to remember the objects.

10 **a** What's in your bag? Make a list. Add one thing that <u>isn't</u> there.

b Work in pairs. Guess what <u>isn't</u> in your partner's bag.

A: *What's in your bag?*

B: *Five pens, two computers, an iPod and a book.*

A: *Two computers? They aren't in your bag.*

B: *You're right. They aren't!*

Reading

1 Read the text. What are the names of the people in the photos?

Photo 1: _____

Photo 2: _____

Photo 3: William, _____ and _____

2 Read the text again and answer the questions.

1 Where is Josh from?
2 Who is his wife?
3 Where is she from?
4 How old is she?
5 Is Charlotte married?
6 Is William her boyfriend?
7 Where are Charlotte and David from?

Vocabulary | numbers 11–101

3 🔊 1.31 Listen and repeat the numbers.

11	el<u>even</u>	25	<u>twen</u>ty-five
12	twelve	26	<u>twen</u>ty-six
13	thir<u>teen</u>	27	<u>twen</u>ty-seven
14	four<u>teen</u>	28	<u>twen</u>ty-eight
15	fif<u>teen</u>	29	<u>twen</u>ty-nine
16	six<u>teen</u>	30	<u>thir</u>ty
17	seven<u>teen</u>	40	<u>for</u>ty
18	eigh<u>teen</u>	50	<u>fif</u>ty
19	nine<u>teen</u>	60	<u>six</u>ty
20	<u>twen</u>ty	70	<u>seven</u>ty
21	<u>twen</u>ty-one	80	<u>eigh</u>ty
22	<u>twen</u>ty-two	90	<u>nine</u>ty
23	<u>twen</u>ty-three	100	one/a <u>hun</u>dred
24	<u>twen</u>ty-four	101	one/a <u>hun</u>dred and one

4 **a** Say the numbers.

b 🔊 1.32 Listen and check.

c Work in pairs.

Student A: say five numbers.

Student B: write the numbers.

A: *nineteen, fifty, ...*

Pronunciation | saying numbers

5 **a** 🔊 1.33 Listen. Which number do you hear first, a or b?

	a		b	
1	a	14	b	40
2	a	17	b	70
3	a	24	b	34
4	a	19	b	90
5	a	13	b	30
6	a	55	b	65

b Listen again and repeat the numbers.

6 Read the How to... box. Work in pairs. Ask and answer about your family.

A: *How old is your sister?*

B: *She's twenty-two.*

How to... ask and talk about age

A: *How old is she?*

B: *She's twenty-five.*

A: *How old are you?*

B: *That's a secret!*

Grammar | *to be*: review

7 Look at the text in exercise 1 again and complete the Active grammar box with *to be*.

Active grammar

I

➕ *I'm 25.*

➖ *I'm not 26.*

❓ _____ *I late?*
    Yes, I _____ *.*
    No, I'm not.

He/She/It

➕ *She* _____ *Brazilian.*

➖ *He isn't British. (He's not British.)*

❓ _____ *she Spanish?*
    Yes, she is.
    No, she _____ *./No, she's not.*

We/You (singular and plural)/They

➕ *They're married.*

➖ *We aren't students./We're not students.*

❓ _____ *you her friends?*
    Yes, we are.
    No, we aren't./No, we're not.

see Reference page 27

8 Complete the dialogues with the correct form of *to be*.

1 A: *Are* you married?
   B: No, we _____. We _____ just friends.

2 A: What _____ it?
   B: It _____ a mobile phone.

3 A: Who _____ he? _____ he your brother?
   B: No, he _____. He _____ my friend.

4 A: How old _____ they?
   B: They _____ 45.

5 A: Who _____ you?
   B: I _____ Carl and this is Lena. We _____ from Argentina.

Speaking

9 Work in pairs.

Student A: look at page 112. You are Lola. Answer Ed's questions about your photos. Then ask Ed questions about his photos.

Student B: look at page 117. You are Ed. Ask Lola questions about her photos. Then answer Lola's questions about your photos.

1 a 🔵 1.34 Read and listen to the How to... box.

How to... say email addresses

A: *What's your email address?*

B: *It's jane.smith@email.com*

@	= at
.	= dot
.com	= dot com
–	= dash
__	= underscore

'jane dot smith at email dot com'

b Work in pairs. Ask and answer about your email addresses.

A: *What's your email address?*

B: *It's anna.duda@fxy.pl*

2 a Complete the questions with a word from the box.

address   email   in   old   phone   spell

1   How _____ are you? ☐
2   Are you married or single? ☐
3   What's your _____ number? ☐
4   What's your _____ here in Edinburgh? ☐
5   Where are you from, Anton? ☐
6   Where are you from _____ Russia? ☐
7   What's your name? [1]
8   How do you _____ *Alekseev*? ☐
9   What's the postcode? ☐
10 What's your _____ address? ☐

b 🔵 1.35 Listen and check your answers. Put the questions in the order you hear them.

3 Listen again. Complete the information about Anton.

REGISTRATION FORM

Name:	*Anton*
From:	*in Russia*
Age:	
Married:	*No*
Address:	*Street , EH3*
Phone number:	*07853*
Email address:	

4 Practise asking the questions in exercise 2a.

5 a Complete the form for you.

REGISTRATION FORM

Name:	
From:	
Age:	
Married:	
Address:	
Phone number:	
Email address:	

b Work in pairs. Ask questions and complete the form for your partner.

A: *I'm Marta. What's your name?*

B: *My name's Felipe.*

2 Reference

to be: *you* (plural), *we* and *they*

➕	We**'re** from London. You**'re** late. They**'re** in the garden.	(are)
➖	We **aren't** married. / We**'re not** married. You **aren't** students. / You**'re not** students. They **aren't** here. / They**'re not** here.	(are not)
❓	**Are we** late? **Are you** Italian? **Are they** married?	Yes, you are. / No, you aren't. Yes, we are. / No, we aren't. Yes, they are. / No, they aren't.

Possessive adjectives: *our, your* and *their*

Pronouns	**Possessive adjectives**
We're from Japan.	**Our** favourite city is Kyoto.
You're my friends.	**Your** passports are in my bag.
They're Brazilian.	**Their** father is American.

a/an

We use *a/an* with singular nouns.

a + consonant sound

a brush   a computer   a key

an + vowel sound

an apple   an iPod   an umbrella

Noun plurals

We add *-s* to nouns to make regular noun plurals.

apple	apple**s**
key	key**s**
pen	pen**s**

For nouns ending in *-s*, *-sh* or *-ch*, we add *-es*.

brush	brush**es**
watch	watch**es**
bus	bus**es**

Irregular noun plurals

Note these irregular noun plurals.

one person – two people

one man – two men

one woman – two women

one child – two children

The alphabet

a b c d e f g h i j k l m
n o p q r s t u v w x y z

These letters have the same vowel sound:

/eɪ/	a h j k
/iː/	b c d e g p t v
/e/	f l m n s x z
/aɪ/	i y
/əʊ/	o
/uː/	q u w
/ɑː/	r

Key vocabulary

Family

male	**female**
brother*	sister*
father (dad)*	mother (mum)*
husband	wife
son*	daughter*
grandfather (grandpa)	grandmother (grandma)
boyfriend	girlfriend
uncle	aunt

male or female

friend

cousin

Note: *step-* can go before the words with a *:
step-brother, *step-daughter*, etc

Personal objects

apple   book   brush   business card   camera
computer   iPod   key   mobile (phone)
orange   passport   pen   purse   (train) ticket
umbrella   watch

Contact details

address   email address   home number
mobile number   phone number   postcode
work number

Listen to the explanations and vocabulary.

ACTIVEBOOK

see Writing bank page 121

27

1 Choose the correct words in *italics*.

A: Who (1) *am/is/are* they?

B: They (2) *'m/'s/'re* my friends, Edith and Bart.

A: (3) *Am/Is/Are* they married?

B: No, they (4) *'m not/isn't/aren't*.

A: (5) *Am/Is/Are* you Dee and Kit?

B: Yes, we (6) *am/is/are*.

A: I'm Ron and this is Nina. We (7) *'m/'s/'re* new students.

B: Welcome to the class!

A: (8) *Am/Is/Are* you and Teresa from Spain?

B: No, we (9) *'m not/isn't/aren't*. We (10) *'m/'s/'re* from Argentina.

A: Where in Argentina? Buenos Aires?

B: No, we (11) *'m/'s/'re* from San Juan.

2 Complete the dialogues with the correct form of *to be*.

A: What (1) *are* your names?

B: I (2) _____ Elbanco and this (3) _____ my wife, Katia.

A: (4) _____ you American?

B: Katia (5) _____ American, but I (6) _____ American – I (7) _____ from Mexico.

A: Where in Mexico?

B: Mazatlan.

A: (8) _____ your son and daughter married?

B: No, they (9) _____ .

A: How old (10) _____ they?

B: Zeynep (11) _____ only eighteen and Sami (12) _____ twenty-two.

A: (13) _____ they students?

B: Zeynep's a student but Sami (14) _____ a student – he (15) _____ a teacher.

3 Choose the correct words in *italics*.

1 Is Lisa *they're/their* daughter?

2 I'm Meltem and this is Zeki. *We're/Our* from Turkey.

3 This is Ahmet. He's *we're/our* uncle.

4 Where is *we're/our* hotel?

5 'Who are they?' '*They're/Their* Mr and Mrs Sands.'

6 *They're/Their* taxi is here.

7 Welcome, Mr and Mrs Reed. *You're/Your* room is number 317.

8 Hi. *We're/Our* American. Where are you from?

9 *They're/Their* father is my friend.

4 Label the pictures.

1 *an umbrella*

5 Find three spelling mistakes in each dialogue.

1 A: What's in your bag?

B: A apple, a mobile phone, two brushs and an book.

2 A: What's in your bag?

B: Two cameraes, an MP3 player, an umbrella, two watchs and an passport.

3 A: What's in your bag?

B: A brush, two apples, a iPod, three pens, a purses, two books, my keys, a umbrella and a mobile phone.

6 Write the male words.

1 mother   *father*
2 daughter   _____
3 aunt   _____
4 sister   _____
5 wife   _____
6 girlfriend _____

7 Rewrite the sentences with the numbers in words.

1 I'm 37 years old.

I'm thirty-seven years old.

2 My daughter is 12.

3 His grandfather is 101.

4 'How old is your son?' 'He's 16.'

5 I'm 58.

6 Are you between 35 and 49 years old?

7 He's 11.

Lead-in

1 **a** 🔊 1.36 Look at the words in the box. Listen and <u>underline</u> the stress.

> bank bus stop café car park cashpoint chemist
> cinema clothes shop deli park petrol station
> restaurant shoe shop (train) station supermarket

b Listen again and repeat the words.

2 Match the words in exercise 1a with the photos and symbols A–O.

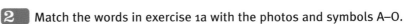

3 Work in pairs.

Student A: point to a picture.

Student B: say the place.

A: *What's that?*   B: *It's a supermarket.*

4 Where can you find ...

1 a coffee? *in a café or a restaurant*
2 a salad?
3 money?
4 chocolate?

5 medicine?
6 a film?
7 cars?
8 shoes?

3.1 | Café culture

Grammar	possessive 's: singular and plural
Can do	order snacks in a café

Reading

1 **a** Look at the photos (A–C) and match them with the countries in the box. There is one extra country.

Egypt ☐   Turkey ☐   Australia ☐   Thailand ☐

b Read about the cafés and check your answers.

Al Samadi

This is Madu. Madu's café is called Al Samadi. It's in Cairo, Egypt. The customers' favourite drink is Turkish coffee with sugar.

B

Cafés around the world

We look at three cafés around the world...

A

Leonardo's

This is Leonardo and this is Leonardo's café. It's called ... Leonardo's! The café is in Melbourne, Australia. The customers' favourite snacks at Leonardo's are prawn salad and chocolate cake.

C

Kulap's food stall

This is Kulap and this is her food stall. It's in a train station in Bangkok, Thailand. What's the favourite snack at Kulap's food stall? It's spicy chicken.

2 **a** Complete the table with information about each café.

	Al Samadi	Leonardo's	Kulap's food stall
Owner			
City			
Favourite snack/drink			

b Work in pairs. Choose a café and tell your partner about it. Use the prompts below.

The café is called ... . It's in ... . The owner's name is ... . The customers' favourite snack is .... .

c Work in pairs. Ask and answer the questions about your favourite café.

1 What's it called?

2 Where is it?

3 What's your favourite snack/drink?

30

Grammar | possessive 's: singular and plural

3 **a** Read the text about Al Samadi again. <u>Underline</u> the examples of 's and s'.

b Complete the Active grammar box with 's and s'.

> **Active grammar**
>
> We use 's and s' to show possession.
>
> **One person (singular)**
> *This is Madu___ café.*
>
> **Two or more people (plural)**
> *The customer___ favourite snacks are prawn salad and chocolate cake.*
>
> **!** **Remember!**
> *It's spicy chicken. = **It is** spicy chicken.*

see Reference page 37

4 Write sentences with the person or people in brackets.

1 (Madu) Amun is his friend. *Amun is Madu's friend.*
2 (Stef) This is her café. *This is Stef's café.*
3 (your parents) Where is their restaurant?
4 (your father) What's his favourite drink?
5 (Ruth) Her mobile is on the table.
6 (Jay) Who is his daughter?
7 (the children) Their pizza isn't ready.
8 (the boys) It's their favourite snack.

Vocabulary | snacks and drinks

5 🔵 1.37 Listen and repeat the words.

1 a coffee
2 milk
3 a prawn salad
4 a cheese sandwich
5 sugar
6 an orange juice
7 a sparkling water
8 a tea
9 a piece of chocolate cake
10 a chicken roll

6 **a** 🔵 1.38 Listen to three dialogues. What do the people order?
1 *chocolate cake and ...*

b Listen again and check your answers.

Pronunciation | /ɒ/

7 **a** 🔵 1.39 Listen. The sound in blue is /ɒ/.
orange chocolate coffee shop doctor

b Listen again and repeat the words.

8 **a** <u>Underline</u> the /ɒ/ sounds.
1 What's the restaurant's name?
2 It's not Jon's cheese roll.
3 Is the chocolate cake in the coffee shop good?

b 🔵 1.40 Listen and check your answers. Then repeat the sentences.

Speaking

9 **a** 🔵 1.41 Read the How to... box. Then listen and repeat.

> **How to... order food and drink**
>
> A: *Can I help you?*
> B: *Yes. Can I have a piece of chocolate cake, please?*
> A: *Eat in or take away?*
> B: *Eat in, please.*
> A: *Sure. Anything else?*
> B: *Yes. A coffee, please.*
> A: *With milk and sugar?*
> B: *Milk, please. No sugar.*

b Work in pairs. Cover the dialogue and try to remember it.

c Change the food and drink and practise the dialogue again.
A: *Can I help you?*
B: *Yes. Can I have a prawn salad, please?*

Vocabulary | adjectives

1 Look at the signs (A–G). What is each sign for?

Sign a is for a café.

Sign b is for a food stall.

2 **a** Write words from the signs next to their opposites. Use a dictionary to help you.

1 slow – *fast*
2 open – _____
3 hot – _____
4 expensive – _____
5 bad – _____
6 old – _____
7 small – _____

b 1.42 Listen and check your answers. Then repeat the words.

3 Find three adjectives in the signs which <u>don't</u> have an opposite.

4 Look at the Lifelong learning box. Read the tip. What is the opposite of *hard*?

Use a good dictionary

! Good dictionaries tell you the opposite of an adjective.

hard /hɑːd/ *adjective*
1 very firm and difficult to cut, break, or bend → Opposite SOFT (1): *The chairs were hard and uncomfortable to sit on.*

Lifelong learning

Pronunciation | /əʊ/

5 **a** 🔊 1.43 Listen. The sound in blue is /əʊ/.

open closed slow no clothes

b Listen again and repeat the words.

6 **a** <u>Underline</u> the /əʊ/ sounds in these sentences.

1 Hello. Is your hotel open?
2 'So, are you Joe?' 'No, I'm Toby.'
3 'What's the hotel's number?' 'It's 0900 485235.'

b 🔊 1.44 Listen and check your answers. Then repeat the sentences.

7 **a** Complete the dialogues with an adjective from exercise 2a.

1 **A:** Hello. Is this shop _____ ?
   B: No, sorry. We're _____ .
2 **A:** Can I have a coffee, please?
   B: _____ or _____ ?
   A: Small, please.
3 **A:** Wow! An Aston Martin. That's a really _____ car.
   B: Yeah! $90,000. And it's very _____ . 200 miles an hour!
4 **A:** Oh, hi! Er ... this is Liv. She's my _____ girlfriend.
   B: Hi, Liv. I'm Emma. I'm Pete's _____ girlfriend.

b 🔊 1.45 Listen and check your answers.

8 Work in pairs. Practise the dialogues.

Grammar | position of adjectives

9 Complete the Active grammar box with examples from exercise 7a.

> **Active grammar**
>
> ***to be* + adjective**
> *We're closed.*
> *It isn't cheap.*
> _____
>
> **adjective + noun**
> *Can I have a small coffee, please?*
> *This is Liv. She's my new girlfriend.*
> _____
>
> ***very*/*really* + adjective**
> *That's a really expensive car.*
> _____

see Reference page 37

10 Put the words in brackets in the correct place.
   good
1 Is it a ⁄ film? (good)
2 Your computer is slow. (really)
3 My iPod new. (is)
4 The chemist open. (isn't)
5 Is he Jen's husband? (new)
6 Can I have a salad, please? (small)

11 Write two sentences for each cartoon. Use the adjective with *very* or *really*.

1 slow
   a Your car *is really slow*.   **b** It's a ... .

2 expensive
   a My hotel ... .   **b** It's a ... .

3 good
   a Is it a ... ?   **b** Is your ... ?

Speaking

12 **a** Choose an adjective to describe your ...
1 house/flat   4 computer
2 car   5 favourite shop
3 mobile phone

b Work in pairs. Tell your partner about your things.
My house is very small but it's nice.

c Tell the class about your partner.
Agata's house ...

Functions	*this, that, these, those*
Can do	ask for and give prices

Vocabulary | prices

1 **a** Match the prices with the items.

b 🔵 1.46 Listen and check your answers.

c Listen again and repeat the dialogues.

2 🔵 1.47 Put the prices (a–h) in the order that you hear them.

a	£17.99 ☐	e	$90.00 ☐
b	$19.00 ☐	f	€16.99 ☐
c	€1.50 ☐	g	€1.15 ☐
d	£2.99 ☐	h	£19.50 ☐

3 Work in pairs. Write five prices and say them. Your partner writes them down.

Listening

4 **a** 🔵 1.48 Listen and look at the pictures. What do the man and woman buy?

b Listen again. How much are the things they ask about?

5 **a** Work in pairs. Read the dialogues in the How to... box out loud.

How to... ask for prices and pay for things

A: *How much is that?*
B: *That's €3.49, please.*
A: *Here you are.*
B: *Thank you. Here's your change.*
A: *Thank you.*

A: *How much is that all together?*
B: *That's £12.50, please.*
A: *Can I pay by card?*
B: *Yes. Enter your PIN number, please. ... Here's your card and your receipt.*
A: *Thank you.*

b Close your books and try to remember the dialogues.

Grammar | *this, that, these, those*

6 Complete the sentences from the dialogues in exercise 4 with words from the box.

> chocolates   flowers   that   umbrella

1 How much is this _____ ?
2 What's _____ ?
3 What are those orange _____ ?
4 How much are these _____ ?

7 **a** Complete the Active grammar box with *these*, *that* or *those*.

b ⊕ 1.49 Listen and check your answers.

Active grammar

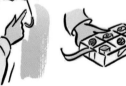

this
flower

_____
umbrella

_____
chocolates

_____
flowers

Note
What's **this**?
~~This is~~ It's an umbrella hat.
What are **those**?
~~Those are~~ They're called 'Birds of Paradise' .

see Reference page 37

8 Choose the correct words in *italics*.

1 What's *that/those*?
2 *This/These* are your books.
3 A: That's £3, please.
   B: £3 for a coffee! *This/That* café is very expensive.
4 *That/These* iPod is Jan's.
5 Who are *those/these* people over there?
6 A: Is your food good?
   B: Yes. *This/That* restaurant is very good.

Vocabulary | colours

9 **a** ⊕ 1.50 Listen and repeat the colours.

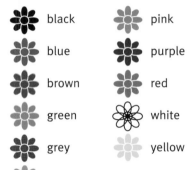

black   pink
blue   purple
brown   red
green   white
grey   yellow
orange

b Work in pairs. What colours can you see in exercise 4?
A: *What colour is that umbrella?*
B: *It's green.*

Speaking

10 **a** Work in pairs.

Student A: look at the flower shop in exercise 4 again. You are the customer. Ask for prices. Use *this*, *that*, *these* or *those*.

Student B: look at the flower shop on page 113. You are the shop assistant. Answer Student A's questions about prices.

A: *How much are those blue flowers?*
B: *They're €2.99 a bunch.*
A: *And how much is this green plant?*
B: *It's €5.50.*

b Change roles and make up new prices.

3 Communication

Can do have a short phone call with a friend

1 **a** 🔊 1.51 Cover the dialogue and listen. Then answer the questions.

1 Where is Nicklas?

2 What is Nicklas's drink?

3 Where is Nicklas's mother?

Nicklas: Hi, Magda.

Magda: Hello, Nicklas. How are you?

Nicklas: I'm fine, thanks. And you?

Magda: I'm OK, thanks. Where are you?

Nicklas: I'm in town, in Spring Park.

Magda: Oh, the park's (1) _____ at this time of year.

Nicklas: Yeah, it's really nice.

Magda: Is it (2) _____ ?

Nicklas: Yes, it is. But my iced coffee is nice and (3) _____ .

Magda: That's good. How's your mum?

Nicklas: Oh, she's (4) _____ . She's on holiday.

Magda: Great! Where is she?

Nicklas: She's in Marrakesh, in Morocco.

Magda: Wow! Oh! I've got to go. See you on Friday evening?

Nicklas: Yes, see you on Friday.

Magda: (5) _____ .

Nicklas: Bye.

b Listen again and complete the dialogue.

2 **a** 🔊 1.52 Read the How to... box. Then listen and repeat.

> ## How to... greet a friend
>
> **Nicklas:** *Hi, Magda.*
> **Magda:** *Hello, Nicklas. How are you?*
> **Nicklas:** *I'm fine/OK/not bad, thanks. And you?*
> **Magda:** *Fine/OK/Not bad, thanks.*

b Work in pairs. Greet your partner.

A: *Hello, Lukasz.*

B: *Hi, Fabian. How are you?*

A: *Fine, thanks. And you?*

B: *I'm OK, thanks.*

3 **a** Work in pairs. Read and repeat the dialogue in exercise 1a.

b Cover the dialogue in exercise 1a and look at the prompts below. In pairs, act out the dialogue.

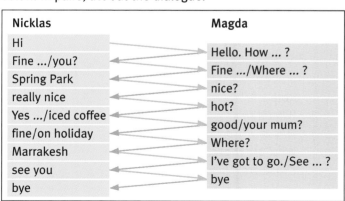

Nicklas	Magda
Hi	
	Hello. How ... ?
Fine .../you?	
	Fine .../Where ... ?
Spring Park	
	nice?
really nice	
	hot?
Yes .../iced coffee	
	good/your mum?
fine/on holiday	
	Where?
Marrakesh	
	I've got to go./See ... ?
see you	
	bye
bye	

4 Work in pairs. Write a new dialogue. Use new people, new places and new adjectives. Practise your dialogue.

Possessive 's: singular and plural

We use **'s** and **s'** to show possession.

Singular (**'s**)

Is it Dong's restaurant?

What are Keira's favourite films?

It's my family's holiday home.

Plural (**s'**)

These are my parents' books.

It's my friends' party.

Where is those girls' mother?

! Remember!

Sometimes **'s** = *is*.

Eric's my friend.

That's a great restaurant.

Position of adjectives

Adjectives can come 1) after *to be*, or 2) before a noun.

1 After the verb

It's really expensive.

His car's very slow.

This café is nice.

2 Before a noun

We use *a/an* or possessive adjectives before the adjective.

It's an expensive computer.

It's a very slow car.

Where's my new pen?

We use *very* or *really* to make the adjective stronger.

*It's a **really** nice sandwich.*

*Her mobile phone is **very** small.*

! Remember!

Adjectives don't change.

He's nice.

She's nice.

They're nice.

this, that, these, those

this/that = singular

these/those = plural

this pen   that pen   these pens   those pens

! Remember!

How much are those sandwiches? = ✓

How much are those? = ✓

Key vocabulary

Places in town

bank

bus stop

café

car park

cashpoint

chemist

cinema

clothes shop

deli

park

petrol station

restaurant

shoe shop

(train) station

supermarket

Snacks and drinks

a cheese/chicken/prawn roll

a cheese/chicken/prawn salad

a cheese/chicken/prawn sandwich

a coffee

an orange juice

a piece of chocolate cake

milk

a sparkling water

a tea

Adjectives

bad – good

expensive – cheap

hot – cold

old – new

open – closed

slow – fast

small – big

fresh

free

nice

Prices

50p = fifty p/fifty pence

50¢ = fifty cents

£2.99 = two pounds ninety-nine

€5.25 = five euros twenty-five

$9.49 = nine dollars forty-nine

 Listen to the explanations and vocabulary.

ACTIVEBOOK

 see Writing bank page 122

1 Write complete sentences with possessive *'s* singular and plural.

1 Claire/computer

It's Claire's computer.

2 the girls/brother

He's the girls' brother.

3 Fred/sandwich

It's _____

4 my customers/favourite snack

It's _____

5 Claudia/parents

They're _____

6 my brothers/friends

They're _____

7 Kimiko/mother

She's _____

8 my friends/cousins

They're _____

2 Is *'s* in the sentences possessive (P) or *is* (I)?

1 Gordon's in the garden.   ☐ *I*

2 Natasha's computer is new.   ☐ *P*

3 This coffee's very hot.   ☐

4 That new café's great.   ☐

5 That is Olga's email address.   ☐

6 His sister's name is Eva.   ☐

3 Put the words in the correct order to make sentences.

1 is free This car park

This car park is free.

2 expensive an computer It's

3 very They big aren't

4 fresh? Are sandwiches your

5 phone a very That's old

6 restaurant is nice This a

4 Change the sentences from singular to plural.

1 This is my phone number.

These are my phone numbers.

2 That's a nice car.

3 Is this your bag?

4 He isn't Sabine's brother.

5 Where is that pen?

6 Is that a new book?

5 Choose the correct words in *italics*.

A: What's (1) *this*/*those*/*these*, on my plate?

B: It's a fish cake.

A: And what are (2) *this*/*that*/*these*, in my salad?

B: They're prawns.

A: And what's (3) *this*/*that*/*those* on her plate?

B: It's a chocolate cake.

A: What's in (4) *this*/*that*/*those* sandwiches?

B: Cheese.

6 Put the letters in the correct order to make drinks and snacks.

1 a efcfeo

a coffee

2 a epiec of loetochca kcea

3 an nogera ueijc

4 a wanrp dasla

5 a pksngialr trwae

6 a eeeshc cnisadhw

7 Complete the dialogues with the opposite of the underlined adjective.

1 A: Is it <u>fast</u>?

   B: No, it isn't. It's really *slow*.

2 A: Is the shop <u>closed</u>?

   B: No, it isn't. It's _____ .

3 A: A <u>big</u> coffee?

   B: No. A _____ coffee, please.

4 A: Is it a <u>new</u> shop?

   B: No, it isn't. It's an _____ shop.

5 A: It's really <u>cheap</u>!

   B: No, it isn't. It's very _____ .

6 A: My coffee is <u>cold</u>.

   B: Really? My coffee is _____ .

A

4

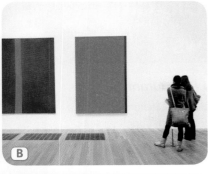

B

C

D

Lead-in

1 a 🌐 1.53 Listen and repeat the words in the box.

> airport   beach   gallery   lake   market   mountain
> museum   national park   palace   river   the sea
> theatre

b Listen again and <u>underline</u> the stress.

<u>air</u>port

2 Divide the words in exercise 1a into two groups.

Nature	City
beach	*airport*

3 Work in pairs. What can you see in the photos? Use the words in exercise 1a.

A: *What's in photo A?*

B: *A beach and ...*

4 What's your favourite beach/gallery/museum/theatre? Ask and answer questions with your partner.

A: *My favourite beach is the beach in Dabki near Gdansk. What about you?*

B: *My favourite ...*

Grammar	*There is/are*; *some*; *a lot of*
Can do	give and understand opinions

Reading

1 Work in pairs. Ask and answer the questions.

1 What is your favourite city for a holiday?

2 What are the top tourist attractions in the city?

2 Read the online guide to Istanbul. Find the names of these places:

1 a palace

2 two markets

3 a museum

4 a mosque

5 a very good restaurant

6 a very bad restaurant

Vocabulary | adjectives of opinion

3 a Read the text again. Which words and phrases in the box can you find?

> <u>aw</u>ful   fan<u>tas</u>tic   great   nice   not bad
> not very good   OK   te<u>rri</u>ble

b Match the words in the box with the symbols.

★ ★ ★ ★ ★   *great*   _____

★ ★ ★ ★ ☆   _____

★ ★ ★ ☆ ☆   _____   _____

★ ★ ☆ ☆ ☆   _____

★ ☆ ☆ ☆ ☆   _____   _____

☐ **top** spots

Istanbul:
Restaurants in The Old City

REVIEWS

Topkapı Restaurant

I think Topkapı Restaurant is OK. The food is not bad, but I don't think it's very cheap.

★ ★ ★ ☆ ☆ *Tansu Yildirim*

Hayat Restaurant

There are a lot of good restaurants in The Old City, but I think this restaurant is fantastic. The food isn't very expensive and it's very nice. Five stars!

★ ★ ★ ★ ★ *Jennifer Luz*

Mevlana Restaurant

There are some bad restaurants in Istanbul and there are a lot of good restaurants. I think Mevlana Restaurant is awful. It's expensive and the food is terrible.

★ ☆ ☆ ☆ ☆ *Mi Sun Kim*

Welcome	Top spots	Essentials	Help	Favourites

Istanbul: The Old City

BASIC INFORMATION

Istanbul is a very big city on the Bosphorus, but a lot of the tourist attractions are in a small area called 'The Old City'. There is a palace (Topkapı Palace), a nice park and a beautiful mosque (The Blue Mosque). There are some great museums and there are two fantastic markets: the Grand Bazaar and the Spice Market. There is also Aya Sofya. These days it's a museum, but it's really an old church. Its dome roof is 30 metres wide.

Click for more information

Topkapı Palace

Aya Sofya

The Blue Mosque

4 Read the How to... box. Then answer the questions and give your opinion. Use the adjectives from the box in exercise 3a.

> ### How to... give an opinion
>
> *I think/don't think* + subject + verb
> *I think this restaurant is fantastic.*
> *I think this place is awful.*
> *I don't think it's very cheap.*

1 What are the top tourist attractions in your town or city? Are they good or bad?

I think the Guggenheim is a fantastic tourist attraction.

2 Which restaurants/cafés are really good? Which restaurants/cafés aren't very good?

I don't think Gino's Café is very nice. The food is very expensive.

Grammar | *there is/are; some; a lot of*

5 **a** Read the text in exercise 2 again and complete the Active grammar box with *is* or *are*.

b 🔊 1.54 Listen and check your answers.

> ### Active grammar
>
> **Singular**
>
> There _____ ('s) a palace.
>   a beautiful mosque.
>
> **Plural**
>
> There _____ some great museums.
>   two fantastic markets.
>
> **some and a lot of**
> We use *there are* + *some/a lot of* + plural nouns.
> *There are some fantastic shops.*
> *There are a lot of good restaurants.*

see Reference page 47

6 Match the sentences with the pictures.

1 There are some people in the theatre. ☐
2 There are a lot of people in the theatre. ☐
3 There's one person in the theatre. ☐

7 Complete the sentences with *There's a/an*, *There are some* or *There are a lot of*.

1 _____ big beaches in Barcelona. (4)
2 _____ restaurants in London. (6,000)
3 _____ famous mountain near Tokyo. (1)
4 _____ national parks in Brazil. (57)
5 _____ parks in New York. (146)
6 _____ palace in Hanoi, Vietnam. (1)
7 _____ great theatres in Warsaw. (10)
8 _____ lakes in The Lake District in England. (88)

8 Look at the map of Los Angeles and complete the description.

66 Los Angeles is my favourite city for a holiday. (1) *There are some* nice beaches and (2) _____ _____ beautiful lake. (3) _____ also _____ mountain. It's called Mount San Antonio. (4) _____ _____ _____ _____ _____ tourist attractions in the city, too. (5) _____ _____ zoo, a park and the famous Chinese theatre. (6) _____ _____ _____ great museums and (7) _____ _____ also two markets. 99

Speaking

9 **a** Work in pairs. Choose a holiday city to talk about. What are the tourist attractions in the city? Make a list.

b Present your holiday city to other students in the class.

Budapest is a great city for a holiday. There are a lot of tourist attractions. There's a river (the River Danube) and there are ...

c Vote for the best holiday city from the presentations.

Reading

1 a Are you a good Tourist Information Officer for your town? Answer the questions.

1 What is the top tourist attraction?
2 Where are the best cheap restaurants?
3 Is there a Tourist Information Office in your town? Where is it?

b Work in pairs. Compare your answers.

2 a Read the text. Match the questions (1–4) with the answers (A–D).

1 Where is it at the moment?
2 What is that strange thing in the photo?
3 Are there any more Info-Bikes?
4 What is an Info-Bike?

b Where is the Info-Bike on the map: 1, 2 or 3?

Vocabulary | prepositions of place

3 Match the prepositions in the box with the pictures (a–g).

in ☐   in front of ☐   near ☐   next to ☐
on ☐   opposite ☐   under ☐

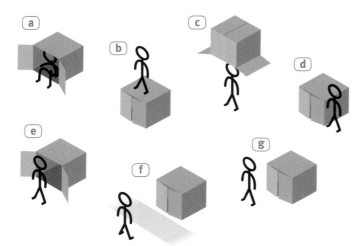

4 Look at the map and choose the correct words in *italics*.

1 Bike 1 is *in front of/opposite* Waterloo Station, *under/on* Waterloo Road.
2 Bike 2 is *near/next to* the Royal Festival Hall, *in front of/under* the NFT.
3 Bike 3 is *in/on* Jubilee Gardens and *opposite/next to* the London Eye.
4 Waterloo East is *opposite/next to* Waterloo Station.
5 There is a car park *in front of/on* Belvedere Street.

The ℹnfo-Bike

A ___2___
It's an Info-Bike.

B _____
It's a small Tourist Information Office – on a bike! In some parts of London there aren't any Tourist Information Offices. The Info-Bike is good for those places at weekends in the summer and at Easter.

C _____
It's in front of the National Theatre, under Waterloo Bridge (near the London Eye). The Tourist Information Officer today is Dave.

D _____
Yes, there are. There are two more Info-Bikes in London.

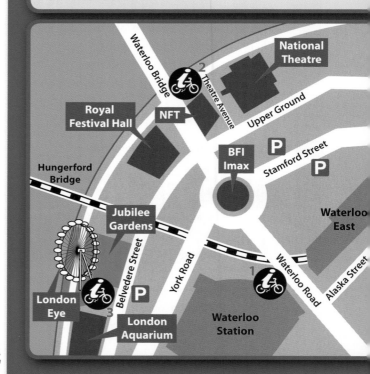

South Bank, Bankside and London Bridge InfoBikes, photography by Libera PR, southbanklondon.com

Listening

5 **a** ⊕ 1.55 Listen. Dave, the Tourist Information Officer answers questions from five tourists. What does each tourist want?

1 *The National Theatre*

b Listen again. Write the dialogue number (1–5) next to the sentences.

a 'Is there a café near here?' 'Yes, there is.' ☐
b 'Are there any museums near here?'
'No, there aren't, I'm afraid.' ☐
c 'Is the National Theatre near here?' 'Yes, it is.' ☐
d 'Are there any car parks near here?' 'Yes, there are.' ☐
e 'Is there a cashpoint near here?' 'No, there isn't.' ☐

Pronunciation | /θ/ and /ð/

6 **a** ⊕ 1.56 Listen and repeat the words.

/θ/ think three thirty theatre
/ð/ there this the that mother

b Underline the /θ/ sounds. Circle the /ð/ sounds. Then say the sentences.

1 That's three pounds thirty, please. Thank you.
2 This is my brother and that's my father.
3 'Are there any nice clothes in that shop?' 'Yes, there are.'

c ⊕ 1.57 Listen, check and repeat.

Grammar | There isn't/aren't; Is/Are there ...?; any

7 **a** Look at exercise 5b again and complete the Active grammar box.

b ⊕ 1.58 Listen and check your answers.

Active grammar

Singular	Plural
⊖ There isn't a bank near here.	There aren't any free car parks.
❓ _____ there a cashpoint near here?	_____ there any museums near here?
Yes, there _____ . No, there _____ .	Yes, there _____ . No, there _____ .

Any

We use *There aren't/Are there + any*.
'Are there any car parks near here?' 'No, there aren't.'
There aren't any museums near here.

see Reference page 47

8 Complete the sentences.

1 *There aren't* any theatres in my home town.
2 '_____ _____ a museum in your town?' 'Yes, there _____ .'
3 'Are _____ _____ shops near here?' 'No, there _____ .'
4 _____ _____ a supermarket on York Road, it's on Park Street.
5 _____ aren't _____ mountains in Holland.
6 '_____ there _____ beach near your holiday home?' 'Yes, _____ is.'

Speaking

9 **a** ⊕ 1.59 Listen and complete the How to... box.

How to... ask where a place is

A: *Excuse me, is the National Theatre (1) _____ here?*
B: *Yes, it is. It's just (2) _____ there.*
A: *And are there any cafés near (3) _____ ?*
B: *Yes, there are. There's a café in the theatre.*
A: *(4) _____ . Thank you very much.*
B: *You're (5) _____ .*

b Use the prompts to make dialogues to ask where places are.

1 A: a restaurant/in this hotel?
B: Yes/over there.
A: any cafés/near the hotel?
B: Yes/a café opposite the hotel.
2 A: a train station/in your town?
B: Yes/near the bus station.
A: an airport?
B: No.
3 A: a toilet/in this station?
B: No/Sorry.
A: small shops/near here?
B: Yes/some small shops on Bridge Street.

c Work in pairs. Practise the dialogues.

10 Work in pairs. Ask about places in/near your school/town.

A: *Is there a café in this school?*
B: *Yes, there is. It's over there.*

Grammar | telling the time

1 **a** Match the times (1–6) to the clocks (A–F).

1 quarter to six ☐
2 quarter past seven ☐
3 ten to twelve ☐
4 twenty-five past two ☐
5 half past six ☐
6 eleven o'clock ☐

 (A)
 (B)
 (C)
 (D)
 (E)
 (F)

b 🔊 1.60 Listen and check your answers. Then repeat the times.

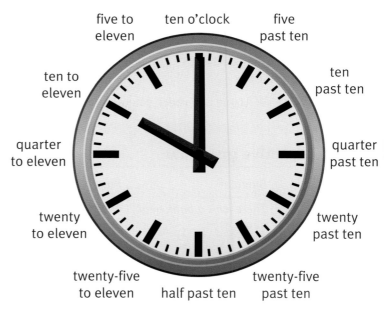

five to eleven   ten o'clock   five past ten

ten to eleven   ten past ten

quarter to eleven   quarter past ten

twenty to eleven   twenty past ten

twenty-five to eleven   half past ten   twenty-five past ten

2 **a** 🔊 1.61 Look at the clock. Listen and repeat the times.

b Work in pairs. Ask for and say the time.

a 18:30	d 11:30	g 06:20
b 17:15	e 19:10	h 13:05
c 20:45	f 19:50	i 09:35

A: *Excuse me. What's the time, please?*
B: *It's half past six.*

Listening

3 🔊 1.62 Listen to two dialogues. Which dialogue matches the photo?

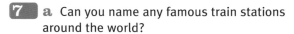

4 Listen again and complete the table.

	Dialogue 1	Dialogue 2
single or return?		
price?		
platform?		
time of next train?		

5 a 🔊 1.63 Work in pairs. Read and listen to the dialogue in the How to... box, then practise it.

How to... buy a train ticket

A: *Can I have a single/return to York, please?*
B: *That's £7.55 please.*
A: *Here you are. What time is the next train?*
B: *It's at 4:45.*
A: *And what platform is it on?*
B: *It's on platform five.*

b Change the information and practise the dialogue again. Use the prompts below.

1 Grand Central Station/$12.50/12:55/8
2 Santa Justa Station/€22.90/15:15/1

Pronunciation | /ə/

6 a 🔊 1.64 Listen and repeat the words.
/ə/ seven under opposite theatre o'clock

b 🔊 1.65 Listen and repeat the sentences.
1 'What's the time?' 'It's eleven o'clock.'
2 Is the theatre opposite the river?
3 Can I have a ticket to London?

c Work in pairs. Read the dialogue out loud.
A: Is that a gallery or a theatre over there?
B: It isn't a gallery or a theatre. It's a museum.

Reading

7 a Can you name any famous train stations around the world?

b Work in pairs.
Student A: read the text below about King's Cross Station. Answer the questions.
Student B: read the text on page 117 about Shinjuku Station. Answer the questions.

King's Cross Station

King's Cross is a big train station in London. It's about 160 years old. The station is open 24 hours a day but the ticket office is open from 05:00 to 01:30. There are about 300,000 (three hundred thousand) passengers every day. There are eleven platforms. King's Cross is also famous for platform 9 and three-quarters from the Harry Potter books.

1 Where is the station?
2 Is it old?
3 When is the station open?
4 When is the ticket office open?
5 Are there a lot of passengers?

c Close your books. Tell your partner about your station.

1 Look at the picture of a hotel room. Do you think it's a nice room? Why/Why not?

I don't think it's a nice room. It's ...

2 **a** Match the words in the box with a–f in the picture.

> blanket ☐   fridge ☐   kettle ☐   shower ☐
> television ☐   towels ☐

b Close your book. What can you remember about the bedroom?

There are some towels on the bed.

3 **a** 🔊1.66 Listen. What do Nikos and Barbara think?

   a   It's great.   **b** It's nice.   **c** It's awful.

b Listen again and complete the information.

		Y	N
1	Double bed?	✓	
2	Towels?		
3	Extra blanket?		
4	Kettle?		
5	Fresh coffee?		
6	Fridge?		
7	Restaurant or café near?		
8	Shop near?		
9	Breakfast time: _____		
10	Checkout time: _____		

4 **a** Look at the Lifelong learning box. Read the tip.

Lifelong learning

> ### Phrases
> ❗ Record new words and phrases in your vocabulary notebook. Use a heading.
>
> **Hotels**
> *a double bed*
> *checkout time*
> *extra blankets*

b Add more phrases from this lesson to the list in the Lifelong learning box.

5 Work in pairs. Roleplay a dialogue between a hotel owner and a guest.

Student A: you are the owner. Copy and complete the table in exercise 3b for your hotel room.

Student B: you are the guest. Ask questions.

A: *This is your room.*

B: *It's really nice. Are there any towels?*

There is/are

Singular

➕
- **There's** *(is) a museum near here.*
- **There isn't** *(is not) a café in this gallery.*

❓
- **Is there** *a supermarket near here?*
  - *Yes, there is.*
  - *No, there isn't.*

Plural

➕
- **There are** *some restaurants near my house.*
- **There aren't** *(are not) any shops near here.*

❓
- **Are there** *any tourist attractions near this hotel?*
  - *Yes, there are.*
  - *No, there aren't.*

some/a lot of/any

We use *some* and *a lot of* in positive, plural sentences.

a lot of = a large number

There are **some** towels on the bed.

There are **a lot of** people in the park.

We use *any* in negative, plural sentences and plural questions.

There aren't **any** good museums in my town.

Are there **any** extra blankets in our room?

Prepositions of place

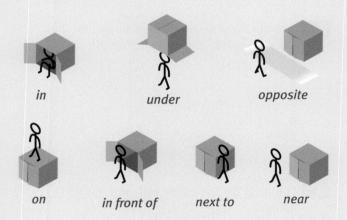

in   *under*   *opposite*

on   *in front of*   *next to*   *near*

Telling the time

A: *What's the time, please?/What time is it?*
B: *It's ten o'clock.*

ten o'clock

half past two OR two thirty

quarter past eight OR eight fifteen

quarter to seven OR seven forty-five

twenty past twelve OR twelve twenty

ten to four OR three fifty

twenty-five past one OR one twenty-five

five to eleven OR ten fifty-five

Note

12:00 in the day = *midday*

12:00 at night = *midnight*

Key vocabulary

Places in the city

airport   gallery   market   museum   palace   theatre

Places in nature

beach   lake   mountain   national park   river   the sea

Adjectives of opinion

☺☺ fantastic   great
☺ nice
😐 OK   not bad
☹ not very good
☹☹ awful   terrible

Hotels

(extra) blanket   double bed   fridge   kettle   shower   television   towel

Listen to the explanations and vocabulary.
ACTIVEBOOK

see Writing bank page 123

1 Choose the correct words in *italics*.

❝My flat is in the centre of town. There (1)*is*/*are* a nice café next to my flat and there (2) *is*/*are* two good restaurants opposite. There (3) *is*/*are* some beautiful buildings in the centre of town and there (4) *is*/*are* a lot of tourist attractions, too. There (5) *is*/*are* a great museum on Wendell Street and there (6) *is*/*are* a gallery next to the museum.❞

2 Put the words in the correct order to make sentences.

1 any your Are theatres town? in there
   Are there any theatres in your town?
2 here. isn't nice There restaurant a near
3 hotel There is house. near my a nice
4 a in Barcelona? there Is beach
5 the in a lot of cinema. are There people
6 aren't here. any banks There near
7 museums Are this near hotel? there any
8 next There this café. is to a chemist

3 Complete the description with the words in the box.

| in   in front of   near   next to   ~~on~~ |
| opposite   under |

There's a woman (1) *on* a bicycle. She's (2) _____ a café. There's a man (3) _____ the café and there's a shoe shop (4) _____ the café. There are two children on the pavement (5) _____ the café. There's a car on the road (6) _____ the woman. The children's football is (7) _____ the car.

4 Write the correct time.

1

`ALARM DATE SET` **06:45**

It's quarter to seven.

2

`ALARM DATE SET` **12:30**

_____

3

`ALARM DATE SET` **09:05**

_____

4

`ALARM DATE SET` **16:15**

_____

5

`ALARM DATE SET` **20:50**

_____

6

`ALARM DATE SET` **07:00**

_____

5 Add the missing vowels to make words. Then mark the words *city* (C) or *nature* (N).

1 p_a_l_a_c_e   [C]
2 b _ _ c h   [ ]
3 m _ s _ _ m   [ ]
4 m _ _ n t _ _ n [ ]
5 t h _ _ t r _   [ ]
6 n _ t _ _ n _ l p _ r k [ ]

6 Complete the dialogues with adjectives of opinion.

1 **A:** Is the gallery n_ice_ ? ☺
   B: Yes, it is. It's f_____ . ☺☺
2 **A:** Are the cafés near here O_____? 😐
   B: They're not t_____ 🙁🙁 but they're n_____ _____ _____ . 🙁
3 **A:** I think she's a g_____ singer! ☺☺
   B: Really? I don't. I think she's a_____ . 🙁🙁

Lead-in

1 a 🔊 1.67 Listen and repeat the words in the box.

> <u>attr</u>active   dark   fair   fat   old   over<u>weight</u>
> short   slim   tall   thin   <u>ug</u>ly   young

b Match the words in the box with their opposites.

attractive – ugly

c Work in pairs. Say a word. Your partner says the opposite.

A: *attractive*

B: *ugly*

2 Choose words from the box in exercise 1a for the people in the photos.

3 a Work in pairs.

Student A: write the names of five famous people. Write one adjective to describe each person.

Student B: match Student A's famous people with the adjectives.

b Change roles. Student B writes the famous people and adjectives. Student A matches them.

4 Describe people in your family.

My uncle is tall and very thin. He isn't very old and I think he's an attractive man.

Grammar	Present Simple: *I* and *you*
Can do	say what you like and don't like

Short and Ugly

Aidan LeBlanc

Listening

1 Look at the photos. The man's name is Aidan LeBlanc. Guess the answers to the questions.

1 Where is he from?   2 Is he single?   3 What is his job?

2 a 🔵 1.68 Listen to an interview with Aidan. Check your answers to the questions in exercise 1.

b Read the questions and answers below. Then listen again and put them in the correct order.

a **Annie:** Do you have any children? ☐
  Aidan: Yes, I do. I have two daughters.

b **Annie:** Do you like your job as a writer? ☐
  Aidan: Well … I don't really work as a writer. It's my hobby.

c **Annie:** So do you have another job? ☐
  Aidan: Yes, I do. I work for an international company.

d **Annie:** Do you like Vancouver? ☐ 1
  Aidan: Yes, I do. I like it a lot.

e **Annie:** Do you like your job? ☐
  Aidan: No, not really!

f **Annie:** Do you live alone? ☐
  Aidan: No, I don't. I live with my wife, Valeria.

Vocabulary | *live, work, have* and *like*

3 a Choose the correct words in *italics*.

1 I *live/like/have* in a big house.
2 I *live/work/like* my job.
3 I *work/have/like* as a singer.
4 I *live/work/have* two children.
5 I *work/have/like* London.
6 I *live/have/like* in Vancouver.
7 I *live/work/like* for an international company.
8 I *live/work/have* two brothers and a sister.
9 I *live/have/like* with my husband.
10 I *work/have/like* in an office.

b Check your answers with your partner. Then say the sentences.

Grammar | Present Simple: *I* and *you*

4 a Look at the questions and answers in exercise 2b. Then complete the Active grammar box with *do* or *don't*.

b 🔊 1.69 Listen and check your answers.

Active grammar

+ I like fresh coffee.
You have two daughters.
I live in a small house.

− I _____ work as a writer.
You _____ like your job.
I _____ live alone.

? _____ you have any children?
_____ you like your job?
Yes, I _____ .
No, I _____ .

see Reference page 57

5 Put the words in the correct order to make sentences.

1 in you office? work Do an
Do you work in an office?
2 live don't near I airport. the
3 three I brothers. have
4 live house? in Do big you a
5 this I like music. don't
6 for company. I small work a
7 like I food. good
8 brothers. any don't I have
9 Do big cities? like you
10 friends you Madrid? any Do in have

6 a Write sentences using the prompts.

1 ***I don't work in an office.*** (not work/office)
2 _____ (like/Hollywood films)
3 _____ (not live/alone)
4 _____ (have/sister)
5 _____ (work/hotel)
6 _____ (live/near the beach)
7 _____ (not like/my home town)
8 _____ (not have/any children)

b Make the sentences in exercise 6a true for you.

I don't work in an office. I'm a student.

7 Work in groups. Look at the pictures. Ask and answer questions with *like*.

A: *Do you like tea with milk?* B: *Yes, I do.*

Pronunciation | /uː/ and /əʊ/

8 a 🔊 1.70 Listen and repeat the words.

/uː/ do two you who Vancouver
/əʊ/ don't so oh euro

b Underline the /uː/ sounds and circle the /əʊ/ sounds. Then say the sentences.

1 'That's two euros.' 'I don't have two euros!'
2 Where are you? Oh! Are you in the museum?
3 Do you like those new students from Vancouver?

c 🔊 1.71 Listen and check. Then repeat the sentences.

Speaking

9 🔊 1.72 Read the How to... box. Then listen and repeat.

How to... show interest

1 A: *I like my job!*
B: *Really? That's great!*
2 A: *I don't like my job.*
B: *Really? That's a shame!*
3 A: *I don't work as a writer. It's my hobby.*
B: *Oh, I see.*

10 a Work in pairs. Do a 60-second interview with your partner. Use the questions in exercise 6a. Show interest in your partner's answers.

A: *Do you live near the beach?*
B: *Yes, I do.*
A: *That's great!*

b Tell the class about your partner.

Marcel lives in an apartment near the beach. He lives with ...

Vocabulary | verbs of routine

1 Match the correct verb phrases with the pictures.

> come home ☐   finish work ☐   get up ☐
> go to bed ☐   have a shower ☐
> make dinner ☐   start work ☐   watch TV ☐

2 **a** Use the verbs in exercise 1 to write sentences about yourself.

I finish work at half past five.
I don't watch TV.

b Work in pairs. Ask and answer questions.

A: *Do you get up early?*

B: *Yes, I do./No, I don't. I get up late.*

A: *What time do you get up?*

Reading

3 Do you have a blog? Do you read any blogs?

4 Read Rebecca's blog. Match the names (Rem, Adam and Frank) with the photos (A–C).

5 Write a tick (✓) or cross (✗) for each person.

Rem:	fruit ✓	salad ☐	TV ☐
Adam:	gym ☐	shower ☐	coffee ☐
Frank:	lunch ☐	gym ☐	work ☐

6 Who are you like – Rem, Adam or Frank?

Rebecca Aalberts
A blog about me, myself and I

SUBSCRIBE FOR FREE 🔊
ENTER YOUR EMAIL ADDRESS
[   ] Subscribe

SEARCH
Search 🔍

SOCIAL MEDIA digg t f

Are my best friends REALLY my best friends?

I think Rem, Adam and Frank are my best friends. But are they really my best friends?

Rem
Rem is a health freak. He gets up early every day. He doesn't have a coffee for breakfast – he has fruit. He has a salad for lunch and he goes to the gym in the evening. He doesn't watch TV. He's very busy and he doesn't have a lot of time for me.

Adam
Adam's my husband. He's a couch potato. He doesn't get up early and he doesn't go to the gym. He has a shower around nine o'clock then he has three cups of coffee and he goes to work. He doesn't make dinner in the evening. I do that. He just watches TV. Does he love me????

Frank
Frank is my brother. He's a workaholic. He starts work around seven o'clock in the morning. He doesn't have lunch and he finishes work at eight o'clock in the evening. Then he goes to the gym, comes home, makes dinner and goes to bed. Does Frank work at weekends? Yes, he does. Does he have time for me? No, he doesn't.
Perhaps my best friend is my teddy bear. It doesn't make dinner but it has a lot of time for me!!!

Posted Wednesday 4th April

Grammar | Present Simple: *he*, *she* and *it*

7 a Read the sentences from Rebecca's blog then complete the Active grammar box with *does* or *doesn't*.

1 Rem gets up early every day.
2 Adam doesn't go to the gym.
3 Frank finishes work at eight o'clock in the evening.
4 Does Frank work at weekends?

b 🔊 1.73 Listen and check your answers.

> **Active grammar**
>
> ⊕ He starts work early.
> She finishes work late.
>
> ⊖ He _____ watch TV.
> She _____ have a lot of time for me.
>
> ? _____ he have time?
> _____ he love coffee?
> Yes, he _____ .
> No, he _____ .
>
> **Note:** *He has a shower.* NOT ~~He haves a shower.~~

see Reference page 57

8 Complete the text with the correct form of the verbs in the box.

> eat   finish   get   have   start   watch   ~~work~~

66 My best friend, Yasmin, is a chef in a Spanish restaurant. She (1) *works* in the evening so she (2) _____ up around eleven o'clock in the morning. She (3) _____ breakfast and lunch together – it's called 'brunch'. Then she (4) _____ TV and (5) _____ work around four o'clock in the afternoon. She (6) _____ dinner at work. Yasmin (7) _____ work around midnight. She works a lot. I don't see her much! 99

9 a Write complete conversations.

1 he have any children // no/want any children
   A: *Does he have any children?*
   B: *No, he doesn't. He doesn't want any children.*
2 she watch a lot of TV? // no/not have a TV
3 he eat fruit? // no/not like fruit
4 she start work early? // no/not get up early
5 he come home early? // no/not finish work early
6 she work in an office? // no/not have a job

b Work in pairs. Ask and answer the questions in exercise 9a about your best friend.

A: *Does your best friend have any children?*
B: *Yes, he does. He has a son and a daughter.*

Pronunciation | /s/, /z/ and /ɪz/

10 a 🔊 1.74 Listen and repeat the words.

/s/   works   gets   likes   eats
/z/   goes   lives   has   does
/ɪz/   finishes   watches

b 🔊 1.75 Practise saying the sentences. Then listen, check and repeat.

1 'Does she work here?' 'Yes, she does.'
2 He likes food and he works in a restaurant.
3 She finishes work then she watches TV.

Speaking

11 a Think of a friend who is a health freak, a couch potato or a workaholic. Write his/her name.

b What is his/her daily routine? Write some sentences.

He gets up around six o'clock every day.

c Tell your partner about your friend.

My friend Sanjay is a workaholic. He gets up at ...

5.3 Making friends

Grammar	Present Simple: *you* (plural), *we* and *they*; *Wh-* questions
Can do	ask and answer simple questions about your life

Vocabulary | days of the week

1 **a** 🔊 1.76 Listen and repeat the times of day and the days of the week.

> **Times of day**
> <u>mor</u>ning   after<u>noon</u>   <u>eve</u>ning   night
> **Days of the week**
> **week<u>days</u>:** <u>Mon</u>day   <u>Tues</u>day   <u>Wednes</u>day   <u>Thurs</u>day   <u>Fri</u>day
> **the weekend:** <u>Satur</u>day   <u>Sun</u>day
> **Note**
> **in** the morning/afternoon/evening
> **on** Saturday/Wednesday/weekdays
> **at** night/the weekend

b Work in pairs. When do you do these activities?

> get up late   go to bed late   go to the gym
> have a shower   watch TV

I get up late on Saturday and Sunday mornings.

In Brazil

In the UK

Reading

2 **a** Look at the photos and guess the answer to the question.

What is the problem for Flavia and her husband, Joe?

b Read the text and check your answer.

c Read the text again. Are the sentences true (T) or false (F)?

1   Flavia is American. ☐
2   Flavia doesn't work on Sundays. ☐
3   Flavia and her husband have a lot of friends. ☐
4   Ricky doesn't have a job. ☐
5   Michael doesn't go out at the weekend. ☐
6   Della has a lot of friends. ☐

Flavia

Wall   Info   Photos

Write something …

Attach   Share

Flavia5
Please help! My name's Flavia. I'm Brazilian and my husband is from the USA. We live in the UK now and we work from Monday to Friday. We're nice people but we don't have a lot of friends here in London. How do we make friends with British people? Are they all 'cold'?

5 July at 21:02 · Comment · Like

3 people like this

Ricky
Hi Flavia
Where do you and your husband work? I'm British. A lot of British people make friends at work. Do you say hello and have a coffee with your work friends? Do you call your work friends at the weekend? My best friends are my work friends.
21:36

Michael_S
You and your husband work on weekdays. What do you do at the weekend? My wife and I are British. We don't stay at home and surf the Internet. We go out and eat good food in restaurants and make friends in pubs and bars.
22:04

Della
Hi Flavia – The British aren't cold but they don't make friends with strangers on the street. My husband and I play sports and we study Italian. We make friends in the gym and the classroom.
22:34

Vocabulary | verb collocations

3 **a** Match a verb from column A with a word or phrase in column B. Use the text to help you.

A	B
call	a language
eat	sport
make	hello
play	at home
say	the Internet
stay	fish
study	friends
surf	your friends

b 🔊 1.77 Listen and check your answers. Then repeat the collocations.

4 Write some advice for Flavia.

Flavia, don't stay at home at the weekend. Play a sport or study a language ...

Grammar 1 | Present Simple: *you* (plural), *we* and *they*

5 Read the Active grammar box. Then correct the sentences (1–4).

1 We plays football on Saturdays.
2 Does you like parties?
3 They doesn't say hello.
4 Do yous eat chicken?

Active grammar

⊕ | You/We/They live in the UK.

⊖ | You/We/They don't make friends with strangers.

❓ | Do you/we/they go to parties?
    Yes, you/we/they do.
    No, you/we/they don't.

---

see Reference page 57

6 Work in pairs. Make sentences about you and your partner.

1 work at weekends   4 play sports
2 live near this school 5 eat chocolate
3 like Mondays   6 get up late at weekends

We don't work at weekends.

Grammar 2 | Wh- questions

7 Complete the Active grammar box with *Where*, *When*, *How*, *What* and *Who*.

Active grammar

A: _____ sports do you play? B: *We play basketball.*

A: _____ do you work? B: *I work in a theatre.*

A: _____ do you work with? B: *I work with English people.*

A: _____ do you go out? B: *We go out in the evenings.*

A: _____ do I make friends with British people? B: *Play a sport or study a language.*

---

see Reference page 57

8 Put the words in the correct order to make questions.

1 do play? sports What you
2 a café? you What drink in do
3 live? you do Where
4 make in your do How country? you friends
5 do What do weekend? you the at
6 Who live with? you do
7 weekend? at the you up get do When
8 you weekdays? to bed do When on go

Pronunciation | *do* in *Wh*- questions

9 **a** 🔊 1.78 Listen. *Do* is not stressed in *Wh*-questions. It is pronounced /də/.

1 Where do you work?
2 What do you eat?
3 When do you get up?
4 How do you make friends?
5 Who do you work with?

b Listen again and repeat the sentences.

10 Work in pairs. Ask and answer the questions in exercises 8 and 9a.

1 Describe the man and woman in the picture.

He's tall and dark. He's ...

2 a 🔊 1.79 Listen and answer the questions.

1 What is the woman's job?

2 What is the man's job?

b Listen again and complete the table.

	Man	Woman
Name	*Katashi*	
Works		
Weekends		

3 Complete the questions from the dialogue.

1 Is the food *nice*?

2 How _____ _____ know Paul?

3 What _____ you _____ ?

4 Where _____ you _____ ?

5 _____ you _____ to a lot of parties?

6 What _____ you _____ at the weekend?

4 Look at the Lifelong learning box. Read the tip.

Use your memory

❗ Memorise short conversations. It helps to remember grammar and vocabulary.

A: *How do you know Peter?*

B: *We work together.*

A: *Really? What do you do?*

Lifelong learning

5 Work in pairs. Try to remember the dialogue in exercise 2a. Check on page 138.

6 Read the How to... box. Then write more questions for part 3 of the box.

How to... start and continue a conversation

1	Ask a general question OR make a comment	*Is the food nice?* *How do you know Paul?* *I like your bag.*
2	THEN introduce yourself	*My name is Katashi, by the way.*
3	THEN ask about work or free time	*Where do you work?* *Do you play any sports?* _____ _____

7 a Look at the photos. Think of general questions to start a conversation.

b Work in pairs. Start and continue a conversation for each picture.

Present Simple

Positive

I You	live work	
He She It	lives works	in London. with two friends. next to a theatre.
You (plural) We They	live work	

We add -s to the verb for *he, she* and *it*.

We add -es to verbs ending in *-ch, -sh, -ss* and *-o*:

She watches TV.

He finishes work at 3:30.

Have is irregular:

She has a good job.

They have a lot of friends.

Negative

I You	don't		
He She It	doesn't	like watch	sport. TV. Hollywood films.
You (plural) We They	don't		

Yes/No questions

Do	I you		
Does	he she it	get up finish work	early? late? before 8 o'clock?
Do	you we they		

Wh- questions

We use *Who ...?* for people (and sometimes for companies).

Who lives here?

Who do you work for?

We use *Where ...?* for places.

Where does she live?

Where are you from?

We use *What ...?* for things and activities.

What is that?

What do you do?

We use *When ...?* for times. (We also use *What time ...?*)

When do you work?

When is her birthday?

We use *How ...?* to ask the way, the amount, the age, etc.

How do I make friends with English people?

How old are you?

How much is that?

Key vocabulary

Adjectives of appearance

attractive   dark   fair   fat   old   overweight   short   slim   tall   thin   ugly   young

Phrases with *have, like, live* and *work*

have breakfast/a brother and a sister/children/a coffee/dinner/friends/lunch/a salad for lunch/a shower

like a city/your job

live alone/in a big house/in a city/with your friends

work as a singer/for a big company/in an office

Verb collocations

call a friend   come home   eat food   finish work
get up   go shopping   go to bed   go to the gym
go to work   make a coffee   make breakfast
make dinner   make friends   make lunch   play sport
say hello   start work   stay at home
study a language   surf the Internet   watch TV

Times of day

morning   afternoon   evening   night

Days of the week

Weekdays Monday   Tuesday   Wednesday
Thursday   Friday
The weekend Saturday   Sunday

Note:

in the morning/afternoon/evening

on Saturday/Wednesday/weekdays

at night/the weekend

Listen to the explanations and vocabulary.

ACTIVEBOOK

see Writing bank page 124

5 Review and practice

1 Write complete dialogues with *you* and *I*.

1 A: live near the airport?
  B: no/live near the station

  A: *Do you live near the airport?*
  B: *No, I don't. I live near the station.*

2 A: like football?
  B: yes/all sports

3 A: work in an office?
  B: no/work in a shop

4 A: have any brothers or sisters?
  B: yes/have two brothers and a sister

5 A: live alone?
  B: no/live with my wife

2 Put the verbs in brackets into the correct form.

From: julia@lemon.co.uk
To: victorbanks@netmail.com
Subject: my new flatmate!

Hi Victor

How are you? I'm fine, but my new flatmate is a problem. His name is Oscar. He's an artist. He (1) *gets* (get/✓) up at 11 o'clock every day. He (2) _____ (have/✗) a shower, but he (3) _____ (watch/✓) TV for two or three hours. He (4) _____ (start/✓) work at about two o'clock in the afternoon. He (5) _____ (work/✗) in an office – he (6) _____ (work/✓) from home. He (7) _____ (finish/✓) work at about six o'clock. That's just four hours! He (8) _____ (go/✓) to bed at three o'clock in the morning.

What can I do?

Love,

Julia

3 Write complete sentences.

1 they/eat a lot of chocolate (✓)
They eat a lot of chocolate.

2 you and Tim/live in the city (?)
Do you and Tim live in the city?

3 Yuri and I/play sport (✗)

4 Ella and Greg/call their friends (?)

5 we/make friends at work (✓)

6 you/work for a small company (?)

7 they/stay at home at the weekend (✗)

8 Nora and I/like Jerry and Michaela (✓)

4 Complete the dialogue with the correct form of the verbs in brackets.

A: Hello, I work *for Life and Health Magazine*. Can I ask you some questions?

B: Yes, OK.

A: (1) *Do* you *live* alone? (live)

B: No, I (2) _____ . I (3) _____ (live) with my friends Jake and Evan.

A: (4) _____ you _____ (eat) a lot of pizza and burgers?

B: I (5) _____ _____ (not eat) junk food, but my friends (6) _____ (eat) a lot of pizza.

A: (7) _____ you _____ (play) any sports?

B: I (8) _____ (play) football on Sundays and Jake (9) _____ (play) basketball on Wednesdays. Evan (10) _____ _____ (not play) any sports.

A: (11) _____ you _____ (watch) a lot of TV?

B: Evan (12) _____ (watch) TV every evening. He's a couch potato!

5 Complete the questions with the words in the box.

How (x2)   What (x2)   When   Where   Who (x2)

1 *How* do you eat pizza? With your fingers?
2 _____ do you work?
3 _____ do you start work?
4 _____ old are you?
5 _____ is he? Is he your brother?
6 _____ food do you like?
7 _____ do you do?
8 _____ do you work for?

6 Rearrange the letters to make adjectives of appearance.

1 lgyu
ugly
2 rhtso
3 noyug
4 nthi
5 rctiatveat
6 radk
7 isml
8 eegiwotvrh

7 Match the parts of the collocations.

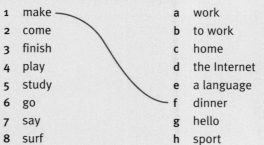

1 make   a work
2 come   b to work
3 finish   c home
4 play   d the Internet
5 study   e a language
6 go   f dinner
7 say   g hello
8 surf   h sport

Lead-in

1　**a**　Match some of the words in the box with the photos.

> bathroom　bedroom　cellar　garage　garden　hall
> kitchen　living room　loft　stairs

b　🔊 2.01　Listen and repeat the words.

2　Work with a partner. Talk about the rooms in your house.

*In my house there's a living room, a bathroom, two bedrooms
and a kitchen. There isn't a cellar or ...*

3　**a**　🔊 2.02　Listen to Marisa and Anya talk about their houses. Match each
person with a photo (A–D).

b　Listen again and choose the correct words in *italics*.

Marisa

❝I live in a small (1) *flat/house* near the centre of town. It's nice, but it's very
expensive. There are (2) *two/three* big bedrooms and the flat is about (3) *sixty/seventy*
square metres. The living room is big, but the (4) *kitchen/bathroom* is small.❞

Anya

❝I live in a small (5) *flat/house*. It's a nice house and it's near a park. There are
(6) *two/three* bedrooms and the house is about (7) *120/130* square metres. The
kitchen and the (8) *bathroom/living room* are small so we keep a lot of things in
the (9) *garden/loft*.❞

4　Write about your home. Use exercise 3b to help you.

I live in a big flat near the train station. It's a nice flat but it's a bit noisy ...

Vocabulary | furniture

1 **a** Match the words in the box with the pictures.

armchair ☐ basin ☐ bath ☐ bin ☐
chair ☐ coffee table ☐ cooker ☐ desk ☐
dishwasher ☐ fridge ☐ lamp ☐ mirror ☐
sink ☐ sofa ☐ table ☐ toilet ☐
wardrobe ☐ washing machine ☐

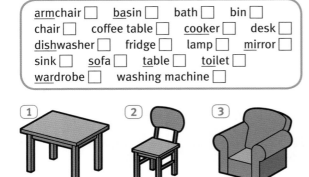

b 🔊 2.03 Listen and check your answers. Then listen again and repeat the words.

c Where do you usually find each item?

You find an armchair in the living room.

2 **a** What are the five most important pieces of furniture in a house? Choose from the words in exercise 1a.

b Compare your list with a partner.

A: *I think a sofa is really important.*

B: *Me too. It's on my list./Really? It's not on my list.*

We haven't got a kitchen!

There are 20 million people in New York, and they all want to live in Upper Manhattan!

A small apartment in Upper Manhattan costs over $1,000,000.

Zaarath and Christopher have got a $150,000 apartment in Upper Manhattan. It's very, very small. It's just 4.5 metres long by 3 metres wide.

Do you like your apartment?

Zaarath: It's perfect. We love it. It's got two windows and I love the views of Manhattan. I've got two cats and they love it, too.

Christopher: We haven't got any children so it's great for us.

Have you got a kitchen?

Zaarath: No, we haven't. We've got a small fridge, but we haven't got a cooker. We eat in restaurants and cafés.

Has your apartment got a bathroom?

Christopher: Yes, it has. But it hasn't got a bath.

Where are your clothes?

Christopher: We haven't got any wardrobes. We collect our clothes from the dry cleaners on the way to work.

Reading

3 **a** Read the text. What is special about Zaarath and Christopher's apartment?

b Read the text again and tick (✓) Yes or No.

Zaarath and Christopher

children	Yes ☐	No ☐
cats	Yes ☐	No ☐

Their apartment

two windows	Yes ☐	No ☐
a kitchen	Yes ☐	No ☐
a cooker	Yes ☐	No ☐
a fridge	Yes ☐	No ☐
wardrobes	Yes ☐	No ☐

4 What do you think of Zaarath and Christopher's apartment?

I think it's a nice apartment, but ...

Grammar | *have got*

5 Read the sentences, then complete the Active grammar box with *have* or *has*.

1 Zaarath and Christopher have got a $150,000 apartment in Upper Manhattan.

2 It's got two windows and ...

3 A: Have you got a kitchen?
   B: No, we haven't.

4 We've got a small fridge, but we haven't got a cooker.

5 A: Has your apartment got a bathroom?
   B: Yes, it has. But it hasn't got a bath.

Active grammar

I, you, we, they

⊕ I've got (_____ got) a sofa.

⊖ They haven't got (have not got) a sofa.

❓ _____ you got a sofa?
   Yes, we _____ .
   No, we haven't.

he, she, it

⊕ It's got (_____ got) a washing machine.

⊖ He hasn't got (has not got) a washing machine.

❓ _____ she got a washing machine?
   Yes, she _____ .
   No, she hasn't.

see Reference page 67

6 Complete the texts with *'ve*, *haven't*, *'s*, or *hasn't*.

❝ I live with my wife in a small house. We (1) **'ve** got a bedroom, a living room, a kitchen and a bathroom. We (2) _____ got a small garden – it's beautiful. But we (3) _____ got a garage.
My wife (4) _____ got a car. She goes to work in the car every day. I (5) _____ got a car, but I (6) _____ got an expensive bicycle. ❞

Chris

❝ I live in my sister's house. She (7) _____ got four bedrooms and two living rooms. She (8) _____ got a TV in her bedroom. She watches TV in bed. She (9) _____ got a TV in the living room but she (10) _____ got a sofa and a big armchair.
She (11) _____ got a big cooker in the kitchen – it's great. We like cooking. She (12) _____ got a microwave oven. She doesn't like them. ❞

Fiona

7 a Work in pairs.

Student A: write five questions about Chris's life. Use *has/have got*.

Student B: write five questions about Fiona's life. Use *has/have got*.

b Ask and answer the questions with your partner.

A: *Has Chris got a garden?*
B: *Yes, he has.*

Speaking

8 a Work in pairs. Guess how many people in your class answer *yes* to the House Survey questions.

HOUSE SURVEY	
1 more than two bedrooms?	
2 a garden?	
3 a garage?	
4 a bath?	
5 a cellar and a loft?	
6 like your flat/house?	

b Do the survey in your class. Check your guesses.

A: *Has your house got more than two bedrooms?*
B: *Yes, it has.*
A: *Have you got a garden?*
B: *No, I haven't.*

Vocabulary | doing housework

1 **a** Match a phrase in the box with a picture (1–9).

clean the bathroom ☐ do the laundry ☐
empty the dishwasher ☐ iron your clothes ☐
lay the table ☐ sweep the floor ☐
tidy the living room ☐ vacuum the stairs ☐
wash the dishes ☐

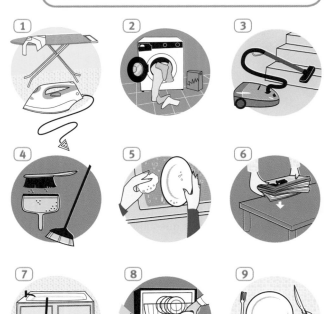

b ● 2.04 Listen and check your answers. Then repeat the phrases.

2 **a** ● 2.05 Listen. Which phrases from the box in exercise 1a do you hear?

b Listen again and complete the How to... box.

How to... make simple requests

A: (1) _____ _____ tidy the kitchen, please?
B: Yes, (2) _____ _____ ./Sure, no problem.
A: (3) _____ _____ empty the dishwasher, please?
B: No, I'm (4) _____ . I can't. I'm very late/tired.

3 Work in pairs. Make simple requests and give answers. Use the vocabulary in exercise 1a.

A: Can you do the laundry?
B: I can't. I'm sorry. I'm really tired.

Who does the

In the UK, men do one hour and 53 minutes of housework every day. Women do two hours and 31 minutes. So what housework do you do? How often do you do it? Couples around the world tell us.

Gabriela: I always do the laundry and vacuum the house. Those are my jobs. Bolivar washes the dishes and he sometimes cleans the bathroom. He never makes dinner. I do that. And I usually tidy the house.

Delun: We never do housework. We're never at home! We have a cleaner! She always does the laundry, sweeps the floor and washes the dishes. JinJing sometimes makes dinner, but we aren't usually at home in the evenings. We eat out.

Reading

4 **a** Read the text and answer the questions.
Who does more housework ...
1 men or women in the UK?
2 Gabriela or Bolivar?
3 JinJing, Delun or their cleaner?
4 Lotta or Viggo?

b Read the text again. What housework does each person do?
Gabriela does the laundry and ...

5 Who are you similar to in the text?
I'm similar to Viggo. We share the housework.

housework?

Lotta:
We both work four days a week so we always share the housework. Viggo usually makes dinner and I lay the table and empty the dishwasher. He cleans the bathroom and I always do the laundry. We do housework in the evening because we're never at home at weekends.

Grammar | adverbs of frequency

6 Read the text again and <u>underline</u> these words and the verb next to them.

always   usually   sometimes   never

7 Read the Active grammar box. Choose the correct words in *italics* in rules 1 and 2.

Active grammar

How **often** do you ... ?

100% ⬉ always
      usually
        sometimes
0% ⬊ never

*I **always do** the laundry.*
*We **usually eat** out.*
*She **sometimes makes** dinner.*
*We **never do** housework.*
*We're **never** at home.*

1 Adverbs of frequency come *before/after* the verb *to be*.
2 Adverbs of frequency come *before/after* other verbs.

---

see Reference page 67

8 Put the words in the correct order to make sentences.

1 always   early.   is   He
2 makes   dinner.   Grandpa   sometimes
3 parents   late?   Are   usually   your
4 never   I   clothes.   my   iron
5 great.   This   always   is   writer

9 a Complete the dialogues with the adverb of frequency and the correct verb.

1 My mum *always does* the laundry. (always)
2 How _____ do you _____ dinner? (often)
3 I _____ _____ my shirts. (usually)
4 Our teacher _____ _____ late. (never)
5 I _____ _____ the bathroom. (always)
6 We _____ _____ the dishes the next morning. (sometimes)
7 They _____ _____ a DVD in the evening. (usually)
8 We _____ _____ the living room at the weekend. (never)

b Write sentences about you. Use the phrases and an adverb of frequency.

1 go to bed early
   I never go to bed early at weekends.
2 eat fast food
3 have a coffee in the evening
4 be late for English class
5 be tired in the morning

Pronunciation | /ʌ/ and /ɪ/

10 a 🔊 2.06 Listen and repeat the words.
/ʌ/ sometimes   does   mum   Monday
/ɪ/ dinner   dishes   living   bin

b <u>Underline</u> the /ʌ/ sounds. Circle the /ɪ/ sounds. Say the sentences.

1 What time does your mum make dinner?
2 I sometimes study Italian in the evening.
3 It's Sunday, so it's Mum's turn to wash the dishes.

c 🔊 2.07 Listen and check your answers. Then repeat the sentences.

Speaking

11 a Work in pairs. Ask and answer questions about the housework in your house.

A: *How often do you do the laundry?*
B: *I never do the laundry. My husband does it.*

b Tell the class about your partner.
Hannah does a lot of housework, but she never does the laundry. She usually ...

Grammar	*like* + *-ing*; *want* + infinitive
Can do	make and respond to offers

Listening

1 Work in groups. Ask and answer questions.

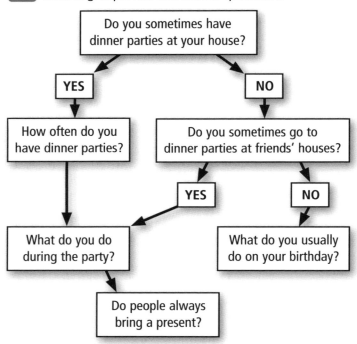

> Do you sometimes have dinner parties at your house?

YES → How often do you have dinner parties?

NO → Do you sometimes go to dinner parties at friends' houses?

YES — **NO**

What do you do during the party?

What do you usually do on your birthday?

Do people always bring a present?

2 a 🔵 2.08 Listen to Ahmad and Jacob. Answer the questions.

1 Why is Ahmad at Jacob's flat?
2 What drinks has Jacob got?
3 What present does Ahmad give Jacob?

b Listen again. Tick (✓) the correct boxes.

		Ahmad	Jacob
1	He likes reading.	☐	☐
2	He likes surfing the Internet.	☐	☐
3	He wants to buy a new camera.	☐	☐
4	He doesn't want to watch TV in the evening.	☐	☐
5	He doesn't like watching Hollywood films.	☐	☐

3 a Read the How to... box and complete the dialogue.

> **How to... offer food and drink to a guest**
>
> A: (1) _____ you like a drink?
> B: *Yes, please. I'd* (2) _____ one.
> A: (3) _____ would you like? I've got ...
> B: *I* (4) _____ _____ an apple juice, please.

b 🔵 2.09 Listen and check your answers.

c Work in pairs and practise the dialogue.

Pronunciation | *would you*

4 a 🔵 2.10 Listen. The <u>underlined</u> sound is /dju:/.

1 Woul<u>d you</u> like a drink?
2 Woul<u>d you</u> like a hot drink or a cold drink?
3 Woul<u>d you</u> like an apple juice?
4 What woul<u>d you</u> like to eat?

b Listen again and repeat the sentences.

5 Work in pairs. Do the roleplay then swap roles and repeat.

Student A: welcome Student B to your house. Offer drinks and snacks.

Student B: you are in Student A's house. There are a lot of CDs and DVDs.

A: *Hi! Welcome! Come in.*

B: *Thank you. Nice house! You've got ...*

Grammar | *like* + *-ing*; *want* + infinitive

6 **a** Look at the sentences in exercise 2b. Complete the Active grammar box with *like* or *want*.

b 🔊 2.11 Listen and check your answers.

> ### Active grammar
>
> ➕ I _____ **watching** TV.
> I _____ **to buy** a new phone.
>
> ➖ I don't _____ **surfing** the Internet.
> I don't _____ **to take** photos with my phone.
>
> ❓ Do you _____ **taking** videos?
> Do you _____ **to listen** to some music?

see Reference page 67

7 Complete the dialogue with *like* or *want* and the verb in brackets.

A: Yes, madam. Can I help you?

B: Yes. I (1) ___*want to buy*___ a new phone. My old phone is very old. (buy)

A: What sort of phone do you (2) _____ ? (buy)

B: I don't know.

A: Do you (3) _____ photos with your new phone? (take)

B: Yes, I do. And I (4) _____ to music. (listen)

A: OK. And do you text a lot?

B: Yes, I do. I (5) _____ . (text) It's fun.

A: And do you (6) _____ games on your old phone? (play)

B: No, not really. The games aren't very good.

A: Some phones have got very good games now. Do you (7) _____ a phone with good games? (buy)

B: Yes. I (8) _____ games on bus and train journeys. (play)

A: So, you (9) _____ a phone with music, a camera and good games. How much do you want to pay? (have)

8 Work in pairs. Write dialogues like the example. Use the prompts.

1 watch TV/with me this evening

A: *Do you like watching TV?*

B: *Yes, I do.*

A: *Do you want to watch TV with me this evening?*

B: *Yes, OK.*

2 listen to music/on my new iPod

3 take photos/of my friends and me

4 play computer games/with me this weekend

Vocabulary | technology

9 Match the words in the box with the pictures.

> camcorder ☐   camera ☐   DVD player ☐
> flat-screen TV ☐   games console ☐
> laptop ☐   stereo ☐   wireless Internet ☐

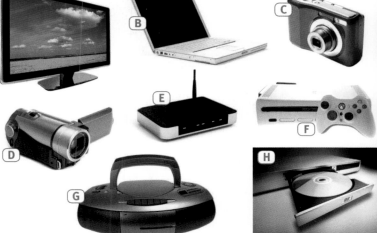

10 **a** Match the two parts of the collocations.

1	listen to	a	video
2	play	b	the Internet
3	surf	c	photos
4	take	d	films
5	take	e	computer games
6	watch	f	music

b Work in pairs. Ask and answer questions about the things in exercise 9.

A: *What's that?*

B: *It's a camcorder.*

A: *What do you use it for?*

B: *You use it for taking video.*

Speaking

11 **a** Work in pairs. Do the technology quiz on page 110.

b What is your score? Who has the top score in the class?

1 Look at the picture and answer the questions.

1 What have the people got in their flats?

He's got a laptop and a stereo.

2 What do they like doing?

She likes playing computer games.

2 **a** 🔊 2.12 Listen to the conversation and look at the picture. Which flat is Helen in?

b Look at the Lifelong learning box. Read the tip.

Listen for important information

❗ When you listen the first time, try to understand the important information. You can focus on the details when you listen again.

Lifelong learning

---

c Listen again and complete the questions.

1 _____ _____ _____ a child?

2 _____ _____ _____ taking photos?

3 _____ _____ _____ playing computer games?

4 _____ _____ _____ a big armchair and a lot of books?

3 **a** Choose a friend in one of the flats. Give him/her a name. Don't tell anyone.

b Work in pairs.

Student A: you are looking for your friend's flat. Answer the doorman's questions.

Student B: you are the doorman. Ask questions to find the correct flat.

A: *Hello.*

B: *Hello.*

A: *Does Kasia live here?*

B: *I'm sorry, I don't know. Has Kasia got a cat?*

A: *No, she hasn't.*

c Swap roles and repeat the activity.

6 | Reference

Have got

Have got means *have*.

I've got a washing machine.

I have a washing machine.

Have got is very common in British English. It is not common in American English.

	I You We They	have got ('ve got) haven't got	a laptop.
⊕ ⊖	He She It	has got ('s got) hasn't got	a camera.

Have I/you/we/they got a garage?
  Yes, I/you/we/they have.
  No, I/you/we/they haven't.

Has he/she/it got a garden?
  Yes, he/she/it has.
  No, he/she/it hasn't.

What have you got in your bag?

Who's got my phone?

Adverbs of frequency

100% always
      usually
         sometimes
0%   never

Adverbs of frequency come after the verb *to be*.

*She's **always** late.*

*They're **never** happy.*

*We're **never** at home in the evening.*

Adverbs of frequency come before other verbs.

*I **usually** empty the dishwasher.*

*Do you **always** make dinner?*

*He **never** irons his shirts.*

We use *never* in positive sentences, not negative sentences.

~~I don't never lay the table.~~ I never lay the table.

We ask questions about frequency with *How often ...?*

How often do you clean the bathroom?

How often does she tidy the living room?

We answer questions about how often with an adverb of frequency or *every + day/week/year ...*

How often do you work from home?

  *I **never** work from home.*

  *I work from home **every week**.*

like + -ing; want + infinitive

When a verb follows *like*, it is usually in the *-ing* form.

*I **like playing** computer games.*

*They don't **like watching** long films.*

*Do you **like taking** photos?*

When a verb follows *want*, it is usually in the infinitive form (*to* + verb).

*They **want to come** in.*

*I **don't want to wash** the dishes today.*

*Do you **want to help** me?*

Key vocabulary

Rooms in the house

bathroom bedroom cellar garage garden hall kitchen living room loft stairs

Furniture

armchair basin bath bin chair coffee table cooker desk dishwasher fridge lamp mirror sink sofa table toilet wardrobe washing machine

Housework

clean the bathroom

do the laundry

empty the dishwasher

iron your clothes

lay the table

sweep the floor

tidy the living room

vacuum the stairs

wash the dishes

Technology

camcorder

camera

DVD player

flat-screen TV

games console

laptop

stereo

wireless Internet

 Listen to the explanations and vocabulary.
ACTIVEBOOK

 see Writing bank page 125

67

1 Complete the email with the correct form of *have got*.

Hi Benita

Thanks for your email. Please come and stay when you are here in Manchester. My husband and I (1) *have got* a flat near the city centre. It's not very big but it (2) _____ (✓) a bedroom for guests. The bedroom (3) _____ (✓) a big bed and an armchair, but it (4) _____ (✗) a TV – sorry! Our flat (5) _____ (✓) a small garden – we share with three other flats – and it's very nice in summer.

We (6) _____ (✗) a car, but I (7) _____ (✓) a bicycle. You can use that.

Look forward to seeing you in the summer!

Anna

2 Write questions and answers using *have got* and the words in brackets.

1 A: *Has your sister got a car?* (your sister/car)
B: *Yes, she has.* (Yes)
2 A: _____ ? (your parents/wireless Internet)
B: _____ . (No)
3 A: _____ ? (you/a games console)
B: _____ . (Yes)
4 A: _____ ? (we/any food in the fridge)
B: _____ . (No)
5 A: _____ ? (Mike/a camcorder)
B: _____ . (No)
6 A: _____ ? (I/a lot of friends)
B: _____ . (Yes)

3 Choose the correct adverb of frequency and write it in the correct place in the sentence in **bold**.
never
1 **I iron my clothes.** I don't like ironing. (always/never)
2 **I cook dinner.** My wife usually does it. (always/sometimes)
3 **My mother surfs the Internet.** She doesn't have a computer. (often/never)
4 They are good teachers. **Their students are happy.** (always/sometimes)
5 **He is tired in the morning.** He doesn't sleep well. (often/never)

4 Complete the dialogue with *like* or *want* and a verb from the box in the correct form.

~~go~~   play   read   stay   surf   watch

A: There's a good film on at the cinema. Do you (1) *want to go* and see it?
B: Not really. I don't (2) _____ films in the afternoon.
A: OK. Do you (3) _____ football? There's a sports centre near here.
B: No, I don't. It's really hot and I'm tired. I (4) _____ at home and just read a book. I really (5) _____ .
A: I don't like reading, but I (6) _____ the Internet. Have you got a computer?
B: Yes. I've got a computer in my bedroom.

5 Match the items (1–10) to the rooms they are usually in (a–e).

1 basin
2 coffee table
3 fridge
4 car   a living room
5 wardrobe   b bedroom
6 sofa   c garage
7 toilet   d bathroom
8 dishwasher   e kitchen
9 bicycle
10 bed

6 Complete the dialogues with the verbs in the box.

clean   do   empty   ~~lay~~   tidy   wash

1 A: Is dinner ready?
B: Yes, it is. Can you *lay* the table?
2 A: Can I have a shower?
B: Yes, but can you _____ the bathroom after your shower?
3 A: There aren't any clean cups or plates.
B: Can you _____ the dishwasher?
4 A: The living room is a mess! There are books all over the floor and the sofa.
B: Yes, it is. Can you _____ it?
5 A: Are your shirts clean?
B: No, they aren't. Can you _____ the laundry?
6 A: Do you have a coffee after dinner?
B: Yes, I do. But first I _____ the dishes.

Lead-in

1 🔊 2.13 Look at the photos. Listen and match a speaker with a photo.

Speaker 1 = photo ____   Speaker 3 = photo ____

Speaker 2 = photo ____   Speaker 4 = photo ____

2 Match four words in the box with the photos.

> aerobics   chess   cycling   exercise   football   a gallery
> puzzles   tennis   a walk

3 **a** Complete the word maps with the words in exercise 2.

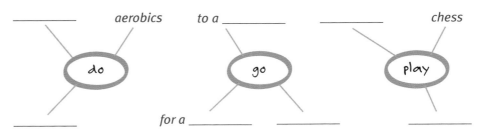

b 🔊 2.14 Listen and repeat the phrases.

c Add more phrases with *go*, *play* and *do* to the word maps.
go shopping

4 Use the phrases to talk about you.
I never do aerobics, but I sometimes go to the gym.

69

Listening

1 **a** Look at the pictures of Eddie and Jo's bad day. Guess the correct order.

b 🔊 2.15 Listen to the dialogues and check your answers.

c Listen again. Answer the questions for dialogues 1–4. Why is dialogue 5 different?

1 Where are Eddie and Jo?
2 What's the problem?
3 What's the new plan?

2 Make sentences about Jo and Eddie. Use the information in exercise 1.

In dialogue 1 Jo and Eddie are in a café. It's cold. They decide to go to an art gallery.

Vocabulary | verbs of like and dislike

3 Put the verbs in order.

> hate   like   love   not like   not mind
> quite like

☺☺☺ _____
☺☺ _____
☺ _____ } films.
☺ _____ } going to the cinema.
☹☹ _____
☹☹☹ _____

4 **a** How do Jo and Eddie feel about these things? Choose the correct verb and write complete sentences.

1 Jo/(love/hate)/eat fast
Jo hates eating fast.
2 Jo/(like/not like)/modern art
3 Jo/(love/not mind)/Jackie Chan
4 Eddie/(like/not mind)/watch vampire films
5 Eddie/(love/quite like)/watch films and eat pizza
6 Eddie/(love/not like)/Clint Eastwood

b Check your answers in the audioscript on pages 139–140.

5 **a** Work in pairs. What do you think of the things in exercise 4a?

I don't mind eating fast.

b Look at the activities on page 69. What do you think of them?

I don't like doing puzzles.

6 **a** Complete the How to... box.

> **How to... make suggestions**
>
> A: *Shall* (1) _____ *go to the cinema?*
> B: *Yes, OK.*
>
> A: *Why* (2) _____ *we go to an art gallery?*
> B: *OK. That sounds nice.*
>
> A: (3) _____ *go and have dinner.*
> B: *I'm not sure. I'm not very hungry.*

b 🔊 2.16 Listen and check your answers. Then listen again and repeat the sentences.

7 Work in pairs. Make and respond to suggestions. Use the phrases in the box.

> do some exercise   go cycling
> go for a walk   go to the cinema
> play chess   play football

Pronunciation | /aɪ/ and /eɪ/

8 **a** 🔊 2.17 Listen and repeat the words.
/aɪ/ like mind bike cycling
/eɪ/ hate play eight take

b Underline the /aɪ/ sounds and circle the /eɪ/ sounds.

1 I like taking photos and writing my blog.
2 I hate cycling in town at night.
3 I sometimes play tennis at eight in the morning.

c 🔊 2.18 Listen and check your answers. Then listen again and repeat the sentences.

Grammar | object pronouns

9 **a** Read Jo and Eddie's sentences from exercise 1. Who or what is the word in **bold** referring to?

1 Chocolate cake isn't good for **me**, but I love **it**.
2 Interesting paintings. What do you think of **them**?
3 The artist is Louise del Monte. Do you know **her**?
4 The signs are very clear. Please read **them**.
5 Clint Eastwood is brilliant. I love **him**.

1 *me = Jo*

b Read the sentences in exercise 9a again and complete the Active grammar box with the words in **bold**.

> **Active grammar**
>
> | Subject pronouns | Object pronouns |
> |---|---|
> | I | _____ |
> | you | you |
> | he | _____ |
> | she | _____ |
> | it | _____ |
> | you | you |
> | we | us |
> | they | _____ |

see Reference page 77

10 **a** Complete the sentences with an object pronoun.

1 Do you like _____ ?
2 Nice phone. I like _____ !
3 I don't like _____ .

4 I hate _____ .
5 I love _____ .
6 I quite like _____ .

b Complete the sentences with an object pronoun.

1 'Do you like big cities?' 'No, I hate _____ .'
2 'Does she like you and me?' 'Yes, she likes _____ .'
3 'Do you know Eva?' 'Yes, I know _____ .'
4 'What do you think of Niko?' 'I like _____ .'
5 'I hate chess.' 'Yes, I hate _____ , too.'

Speaking

11 Complete the table on page 118 for you. Then compare your answers in groups.

A: *I love playing football.*
B: *Really? I don't like playing it, but I like watching it.*

7.2 Amazing abilities

Grammar | *can/can't*

Can do | Talk about abilities

Vocabulary | abilities

1 **a** Match the verbs and phrases in the box with the pictures.

> cook ☐ dance ☐ drive ☐
> play the piano ☐ sing ☐
> speak French ☐ talk to animals ☐
> use a computer ☐
> write computer programs ☐

b 🔊 2.19 Listen and check your answers. Then repeat the verbs and phrases.

2 Work in pairs. Answer the questions with verbs and phrases from exercise 1a.

1 What do you like doing?
2 What do you never do?
3 What do you want to learn to do?

I like cooking. I never play the piano. I want to learn to sing.

Reading

3 🔊 2.20 Read and listen to the texts. Two texts are true. Which one do you think is false?

4 Read the text again. Are the sentences true (T), false (F) or not given (NG)?

1 Kevin lives in Africa. ☐
2 He sometimes kisses lions. ☐
3 Ding Wen uses a computer every day. ☐
4 Ding Wen's father writes computer programs, too. ☐
5 Inna speaks Chinese. ☐
6 Olga speaks Japanese. ☐

5 Who do you want to meet, Kevin or Ding Wen? Give a reason.

I want to meet Kevin. I want to talk to him about his life.

How do they do that?
We talk to four people with amazing abilities!

1 Can people really talk to animals? Kevin Richardson can. Well, perhaps he can't talk to them, but he can understand them. Kevin lives and works in South Africa. He makes TV films about lions and other animals. He can look into their eyes and kiss them on the nose. How does he do it? 'Love and trust,' Kevin says.

2 Can you use a computer? Lim Ding Wen can and he can write computer programs. Ding Wen is nine years old and he lives in Malaysia. In his free time he writes programs for computers and mobile phones. What does Ding Wen's father say? 'It's easy. Everyone can do it.'

3 Olga and Inna Abelev are Russian twins in their 70s. They can speak over twenty different languages. 'I sometimes talk to Olga in Chinese or Korean,' Inna says, 'and she talks to me in French or Italian.' The twins can't speak Japanese. 'I want to learn that next year,' Olga says.

Grammar | *can/can't*

6 **a** <u>Underline</u> all the examples of *can* and *can't* in the text.

b Complete the Active grammar box with *can* or *can't*.

> ### Active grammar
>
> ⊕ | *Kevin can talk to lions.*
> ⊖ | *They _____ speak Chinese.*
> ? | *_____ you write computer programs?*
> *Yes, I _____ .*
> *No, I _____ .*
> *What languages _____ they speak?*

see Reference page 77

7 Complete the real story about Olga and Inna.

Olga and Inna are Russian twins. They are musicians. They (1) _____ (✓/sing) in three different languages and they (2) _____ (✓/play) the piano. They also love dancing but these days they (3) _____ (✗/dance) very much.

The twins are different in some ways. Olga (4) _____ (✓/use) a computer. She's got a laptop and she always has it with her. 'I'm very good at computers,' says Olga, 'but I (5) _____ (✗/write) computer programs.'

Inna (6) _____ (✗/use) a computer. She's got a mobile phone, but she doesn't use it. 'I (7) _____ (✗/understand) it,' she says.

8 Complete the questions and answers.

1 Kevin/understand lions?

Can Kevin understand lions?

Yes, he can.

2 The lions/understand Kevin?
3 Ding Wen/use a computer?
4 He/write computer programs?
5 Olga and Inna/speak Japanese?
6 Inna/use a computer?

Pronunciation | *can* and *can't*

9 **a** 🌐 2.21 Listen and <u>underline</u> the words with stress.

1 <u>He</u> can <u>dance</u>.
2 I can play the piano.
3 They can't sing.
4 You can't use a computer.

b Listen again and repeat. Notice the pronunciation of *can* and *can't*.

Sentences 1 and 2: /kən/

Sentences 3 and 4: /kɑːnt/

c Read the text in exercise 7 out loud.

10 🌐 2.22 Listen. Tick (✓) the word you hear.

	can	can't
1	☐	☐
2	☐	☐
3	☐	☐
4	☐	☐
5	☐	☐
6	☐	☐

Speaking

11 Work in pairs. Ask your partner questions with *Can you ...?* and the verbs in exercise 1a.

A: *Can you cook?*

B: *Yes, I can.*

12 Look at the photo of a personal assistant and the skills he needs. Find the best person in the class for this job.

Personal assistant

Skills

Bonjour!

concert

The 51st State

The 02 Arena   June 9, 10 and 11

play

TALKING TO ANIMALS

by Joleen Miles

Directed by Katie Ormond
Almeida Theatre   March 16th–30th

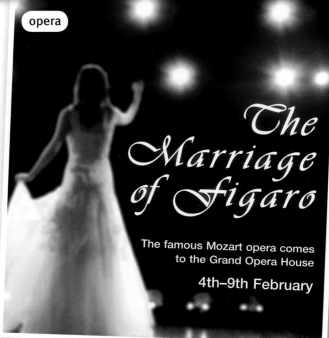

opera

The Marriage of Figaro

The famous Mozart opera comes
to the Grand Opera House

4th–9th February

musical

The High Life

An amazing show!
The Old House Theatre
2nd September– 31st October

Vocabulary | months

1 Look at the posters. Which performance would you like to see?

I'd like to see the opera.

2 **a** Find five months on the posters and put them in the correct place on the list.

1	January	7	July
2	_____	8	August
3	_____	9	_____
4	April	10	_____
5	May	11	November
6	_____	12	December

b 🔊 2.23 Listen and check your answers.

c Listen again and mark the stress. Which seven months contain the sound /ə/?

3 Look at the Lifelong learning box. Read the tip.

Personalise

! Use new vocabulary in a sentence about you. It helps to remember new words.

My birthday is in September.

My sister's birthday is in July.

Lifelong learning

4 Work in pairs and answer the questions.

1 What is your favourite month?

2 What month don't you like?

Listening

5 **a** ● 2.24 Listen to two people make telephone bookings for shows. Which shows from exercise 1 do they book?

Customer 1 = _____   Customer 2 = _____

b Listen again and complete the details.

	Customer 1	Customer 2
Month	*October*	
Doors open		
Time of performance		
Ticket price		

Vocabulary | ordinal numbers and dates

6 **a** Complete the list with the ordinal numbers.

seventh   **eighth**
twentieth   **fourteenth**
sixteenth   **eighteenth**
twelfth   **fifth**
second   **fifteenth**
sixth   **eleventh**
nineteenth   **third**

1st	first	2nd	_____	3rd	_____
4th	fourth	5th	_____	6th	_____
7th	_____	8th	_____	9th	ninth
10th	tenth	11th	_____	12th	_____
13th	thirteenth	14th	_____	15th	_____
16th	_____	17th	seventeenth	18th	_____
19th	_____	20th	_____	21st	twenty-first

b ● 2.25 Listen and repeat the ordinal numbers.

7 **a** Read the How to... box. Then say the dates in the posters in exercise 1.

How to... write and say dates

Write	Say
1st January	*the first of January/January the first*
2nd July	*the second of July/July the second*
3rd April	*the third of April/April the third*

b Write three important dates for you, then tell your partner.

The twenty-third of July is my son's birthday.
The first of May is my wedding anniversary.

Grammar | in, at, on

8 **a** Look at the sentences from exercise 5. Then complete the Active grammar box with *in*, *at* or *on*.

1 Doors open at seven o'clock.
2 There are tickets in October.
3 Have you got any tickets on Saturday 6th October?

Active grammar

____ + months
____ + dates/days
____ + times/*the beginning/the end*

see Reference page 77

b Complete the dialogue with *in*, *at* or *on*.

A: Hello, TicketShop.
B: Hello. I'd like two tickets for *Aida* (1) _____ the 28th February.
A: I'm afraid *Aida* is sold out (2) _____ February.
B: Is it sold out (3) _____ the beginning of March too?
A: No, it isn't. What date (4) _____ March would you like?
B: Have you got any tickets (5) _____ the 5th March?
A: OK. There's a show (6) _____ the afternoon and there's a show (7) _____ the evening.
B: I'd like the evening show, please.
A: OK. Doors open (8) _____ 6:30 and the show starts (9) _____ 7:00.

Speaking

9 Work in pairs. Have a conversation. Use the posters in exercise 1 and the prompts below.

Assistant	Caller
Hello.	two tickets for ...
sold out that month	sold out next month?
what date?	(say a date)
afternoon or evening show?	afternoon
Doors open ... and show starts ...	price?
That's ... (say price and price altogether)	

Can do order food in a restaurant

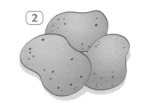

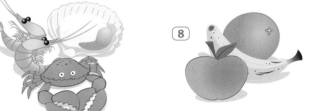

1 **a** Match the words in the box with the pictures.

> beef ☐　cheese ☐　chicken ☐　chocolate ☐
> fish ☐　fruit ☐　lamb ☐　pasta ☐　potatoes ☐
> rice ☐　seafood ☐　vegetables ☐

b 2.26 Listen and check your answers. Then repeat the words.

2 Complete the menu with words from exercise 1a.

TODAY'S MENU

STARTERS
(1) _Fish_ soup
(2) _____ salad

MAIN COURSES
Roast (3) _____ with roast
(4) _____ and vegetables
(5) _____ pasta
(6) _____ chops with rice

DESSERTS
(7) _____ cake
(8) _____ salad
(9) _____ and biscuits

3 2.27 Listen and check your answers.

4 **a** Listen again and put these phrases in order.

a Are you ready to order? ☐
b Can I take your plates? ☐
c And for you, Sir? ☐
d Would you like a dessert? ☐
e Can we have the bill, please? ☐
f Would you like to order any drinks? ☐
g A table for two, please. ☐
h I think I'd like the seafood pasta. ☐
i For the main course I'd like the roast beef. ☐
j Take a seat, please. ☐
k I'd like a sparkling water, please. ☐

b Who says each phrase – the waiter, the man, or the woman?

5 2.28 Listen and repeat the phrases.

6 **a** Choose your favourite starter, main course and dessert from the menu.

b Work in groups of three. Roleplay a conversation between a waiter/waitress and two customers.

Object pronouns

Object pronouns are the object of the verb.
They usually come after the verb. For example:

*He likes **her**.*

He is the subject. *Her* is the object.

Subject pronouns	Object pronouns
I	me
you	you
he	him
she	her
it	it
you	you
we	us
they	them

*Do you like **me**?*
*She lives with **them**.*
*We don't know **him**.*

Can/can't

We use *can* and *can't* before the verb to show ability.

I You He/She/It We They	can can't	cook roast lamb. speak Italian. use a computer. play the piano. sing. dance very well.

Can	I you he/she/it we they	cook roast lamb? speak Italian? use a computer? play the piano? sing? dance very well?

*Yes, I/you/he/she/it/we/they **can**.*
*No, I/you/he/she/it/we/they **can't**.*

*She **can speak** five languages.*
*We **can't speak** German.*
***Can** you **sing**?*

in, at, on

***in** + months*
*My birthday is **in** August.*

***on** + dates and days*
*Are you free **on** 21st November?*
*He doesn't work **on** Tuesdays.*

***at** + times and the beginning/end*
*My train is **at** 4:15.*
*It's **at** the end of July.*

Key vocabulary

Leisure activities

do aerobics   do exercise   do puzzles
go cycling   go for a walk   go to a gallery
play chess   play football   play tennis

Verbs of like and dislike

love   like   quite like   not mind   not like   hate

Abilities

cook   dance   drive   play the piano   sing
speak French   talk to animals   use a computer
write computer programs

Months

January   February   March   April   May   June   July
August   September   October   November
December

Ordinal numbers

1st	first	12th	twelfth
2nd	second	13th	thirteenth
3rd	third	14th	fourteenth
4th	fourth	15th	fifteenth
5th	fifth	16th	sixteenth
6th	sixth	17th	seventeenth
7th	seventh	18th	eighteenth
8th	eighth	19th	nineteenth
9th	ninth	20th	twentieth
10th	tenth	21st	twenty-first
11th	eleventh		

Dates

Write	Say
18th September	the eighteenth of September/ September the eighteenth
24th July	the twenty-fourth of July/ July the twenty-fourth

 Listen to the explanations and vocabulary.

ACTIVEBOOK

 see Writing bank page 126

7 Review and practice

1 Complete each sentence with an object pronoun.

1 She's really nice. Do you like _her_?
2 Lamb chops? Yuk! I hate _____ .
3 I talk to my cat, but it doesn't understand _____ .
4 He's our friend. We like _____ .
5 I love roast chicken, but I can't cook _____ .
6 Are you Ken? Can I talk to _____ for a moment?
7 We want to go for a walk. Do you want to come with _____ ?
8 Helen is on the phone. Do you want to talk to _____ ?
9 They're Betina's friends, Petra and Frank. I really like _____ .
10 What's his phone number? I want to call _____ .

2 Correct the mistakes.

1 I can't to use a computer.
   I can't use a computer.
2 He can plays the piano.
   _____
3 Can she cooks Italian food?
   _____
4 'Can you drive?' 'No, I can.'
   _____
5 We sing can, but we dance can't.
   _____
6 Can drive you?
   _____
7 He's only six, but he cans play golf.
   _____
8 'Can your brother to swim?' 'Yes, he can.'
   _____

3 Complete the dialogues with *in*, *at* or *on*.

1 **A:** When is your holiday?
   B: It's _at_ the beginning of August.
2 **A:** When's your party?
   B: It's _____ Friday.
3 **A:** Are you free _____ 29th October?
   B: No, I'm not, I'm afraid. I'm on holiday.
4 **A:** What time does the show start?
   B: _____ eight o'clock.
5 **A:** Is your birthday _____ September?
   B: No, it isn't. It's _____ November.
6 **A:** When does your new job start?
   B: _____ the end of August.
7 **A:** Is the match _____ Tuesday evening?
   B: No, Wednesday evening.

4 Complete the sentences with *do*, *go* or *play*.

1 Shall we _go_ to a gallery this afternoon?
2 Can you _____ the piano?
3 I always _____ the puzzles in the newspaper.
4 He _____ football for Barcelona.
5 It's a nice day. Let's _____ cycling.
6 I want to go out and _____ some exercise.
7 I sometimes _____ chess with my grandfather.

5 Write complete sentences with verbs from the box.

> don't like   don't mind   hate   like   ~~love~~
> quite like

1 I/☺☺☺/cook
   I love cooking.
2 my brother/☺/listen to my music
   _____
3 you/☺☺/sing
   _____
4 a lot of people/☹☹☹/eat alone
   _____
5 my friend/☹☹/drive
   _____
6 we/☺/play chess
   _____

6 Write the date in two forms.

1 13/11 say: *the thirteenth of November*
   write: 13ᵗʰ November
2 22/08 say: _____
   write: _____
3 11/02 say: _____
   write: _____
4 31/05 say: _____
   write: _____
5 28/01 say: _____
   write: _____
6 02/04 say: _____
   write: _____
7 20/07 say: _____
   write: _____
8 03/09 say: _____
   write: _____

Lead-in

1 **a** Match the years in the box with the photos of famous firsts.

1935 ☐   1946 ☐   1969 ☐   2002 ☐

b 🔊 2.29 Listen and check your answers.

c Listen again and repeat the years.

2 **a** Say the years.

1826   1896   1971   1981   1995   2006

b Match the years to more firsts.

The first eBay auction

The first photograph

The first cashpoint

The first computer virus

The first horror film

The first Blu-ray film

c 🔊 2.30 Listen and check your answers.

3 Work in pairs. Write firsts from your life. Your partner guesses the year.

A: *My first day at university!*

B: *2004?*

A: *No, 2007.*

Vocabulary | jobs

1 **a** Work in pairs. Who are the people in photos 1–11?

A: *I think number one is Grace Kelly.*

B: *Grace Kelly? I don't know her.*

b Match each person with a job from the box.

> actor ☐   artist ☐   business person ☐   dancer ☐   leader ☐
> musician ☐   politician ☐   scientist ☐   singer ☐
> sports star ☐   writer ☐

c 🔘 2.31 Listen and check your answers. Then listen again and repeat the jobs.

2 Complete the sentences with a job.

1 I want to be …
2 I don't want to be …
3 My friend, [name], is …

Reading

3 Read about two 20th century icons below. How old were they when they died?

Vote for your favourite 20th century icons

The 20th century was the first 'celebrity century'. So who were the top icons? We look at some of the big names.

Michael Jackson

Michael Jackson was a singer, dancer and actor. He was born on 29th August 1958, in a city near Chicago. He was the eighth of ten children. His father, Joseph, was a musician in a band called *The Falcons*.

Michael was the singer and song writer for *The Jacksons*. The other singers in the band were Michael's brothers. Their best-selling single was *I Want You Back* in 1969. Michael's 1982 album *Thriller* was number one in the USA for thirty-seven weeks. Michael was married twice. His death, on 25th June 2009, was on the front page of newspapers all around the world.

Grace Kelly

Grace Kelly was an actor and a princess. She was born on 12th November 1929, in Philadelphia. Her first film was *Fourteen Hours* in 1951. She was also in *Rear Window* in 1954 and *High Society* in 1956. Grace and Prince Rainier III of Monaco were married in the same year. After that her name was the Princess of Monaco or Princess Grace. Her death in a car crash, on 14th September 1982, was a big news story.

> *Vote for your favourite icon online at*
> **www.celebritycentury.org**

4 Read the text again and choose the correct options.

1 Michael Jackson:
  a one of eight children **b** one of ten children
2 Michael's brothers:
  a singers in *The Jacksons*
  b singers in *The Falcons*
3 *Thriller*:
  a number one for a short time
  b number one for a long time
4 Grace Kelly:
  a from the USA **b** from Monaco
5 Grace Kelly's first film:
  a *Fourteen Hours* **b** *Rear Window*
6 Grace Kelly and the Prince of Monaco:
  a married in 1954 **b** married in 1956

Grammar | Past Simple of *to be*: positive

5 **a** Underline the examples of *was* and *were* in the texts about Michael Jackson and Grace Kelly.

b Complete the Active grammar box with *was* or *were*.

c 2.32 Listen and check your answers.

Active grammar

I was a student.
You were my best friend.
He _____ the eighth of ten children.
She _____ in Rear Window.
It _____ a great film.
You were Michael Jackson fans.
We were singers.
They _____ Michael's brothers.

---

see Reference page 87

6 **a** Complete the text with *was* or *were*.

Mahatma Gandhi (1) _____ born on 2nd October 1869, in Gujarat, India. At school Gandhi (2) _____ an average student but later in life he (3) _____ a writer, a politician and a great leader. His ideas (4) _____ important for millions of people around the world. In 1999 Gandhi (5) _____ one of *The 100 Most Important People of the 20th Century**. Albert Einstein (6) _____ first. Gandhi and Franklin Roosevelt (7) _____ joint second. Bart Simpson and Bruce Lee (8) _____ also on the list.

* A list by *Time* magazine

b Write five sentences from your answers to exercise 4.

Michael Jackson was one of ten children.

Pronunciation | /ɜː/

7 **a** 2.33 Listen and repeat the words.

/ɜː/ were person thirty first her

b Underline the /ɜː/ sounds in the sentences. Then say them.
1 You were my first love.
2 My daughter is a beautiful girl. This is her photo.
3 They were my first friends. They're about thirty years old now.

c 2.34 Listen, check and repeat the sentences.

Listening

Coco Chanel

8 **a** 2.35 Listen and make notes about some more people on *The 100 Most Important People of the 20th Century* list.

	Akio Moriata	Coco Chanel	Crick and Watson
Job			
Nationality			
Other information			

b Work in pairs and compare your notes. Then listen again and check.

Speaking

9 **a** Make your own list of the top three 20th century icons.

b Find some information about your icons on the Internet.

10 Present your information to the class.

My top three 20th century icons are Eva Perón, Fidel Castro and Martin Luther King. Eva Perón was born in Los Toldos in Argentina in 1895. She ...

8.2 | Memories

Grammar | Past Simple of *to be*: negatives and questions

Can do | give a brief description of a past experience

Vocabulary | past time expressions

1 a Read the quotes (A–D) and match them with the photos (1–4).

A 'I remember my first day at school. It was in 1981. My teacher, Mrs Clark, was really nice, but I was very unhappy!'

B 'I remember my first day at secondary school. It was last year and it was really cool. My best friend, Shelly, was next to me.'

C 'I remember my first day at school. It was sixty years ago, but it seems like yesterday. Time goes so fast.'

D 'My first day at school was yesterday. I was scared yesterday morning, but today I'm OK.'

1 ☐ Rosetta

2 ☐ Jacob

3 ☐ Amy

4 ☐ Liam

b Which words in the quotes tell you the answers?

2 a Read the quotes again. Underline examples of *ago*, *last*, *yesterday* and *in*.

b Complete the time expressions with *ago*, *last*, *yesterday* or *in*.

yesterday
_____ night
_____ morning/afternoon/evening
two days _____
_____ week/month
six months _____
_____ year
_____ 2010
ten years _____
_____ 1980

3 a Change the time expressions to make these sentences true for you.

1 I was late for school/work yesterday.

2 I was really tired yesterday evening.

3 I remember my first day at secondary school. It was twenty years ago.

4 I remember my first email. It was in 1997.

5 I remember my first 3D film. It was last year.

b Work in pairs. Compare your answers.

Grammar | Past Simple of *to be*: negatives and questions

4 Look at the sentences, then complete the Active grammar box with *was*, *wasn't*, *were* or *weren't*.

1 'Was it a small mobile phone?' 'No, it wasn't.'

2 'Was it last year?' 'Yes, it was.'

3 'Were they Spanish?' 'Yes, they were.'

4 Mobile phones weren't cheap then.

5 It wasn't good. In fact, it was terrible.

Active grammar

I, he, she, it

⊖ It wasn't French.

❓ _____ it a good song?
   Yes, it _____ .
   No, it _____ .

you (singular and plural), *we*, *they*

⊖ They weren't cheap.

❓ _____ they expensive?
   Yes, they _____ .
   No, they _____ .

---

see Reference page 87

5 Complete the interview with Jamie, an IT expert. Use *was*, *were*, *wasn't* or *weren't*.

What (1) _was_ your first computer?

My first computer (2) _____ a laptop. It (3) _____ 1995 and laptops then (4) _____ the same as laptops now. They (5) _____ fast and light.

(6) _____ it expensive?

No, it (7) _____ . It was a present from my parents. It was for my brother and me.

(8) _____ you happy with it?

Yes, we (9) _____ . It (10) _____ small, it (11) _____ fast and it (12) _____ beautiful, but we loved it.

6 **a** Work in pairs. Ask and answer the questions about 1995.

1 mobile phones/small // No

A: *Were mobile phones small in 1995?*

B: *No, they weren't.*

2 the Internet/new? // Yes
3 CDs/cheap? // No
4 Microsoft/a big company? // Yes
5 MP3 players/popular? // No
6 you/happy? // Yes

b Ask and answer the same questions about 2010.

A: *Were mobile phones small in 2010?*

Listening

7 Look at the game *I remember my first ...* Which things on the board do you remember?

8 **a** ⏺ 2.36 Listen to Helder, Fran and Don. Which four topics from the game do they talk about?

b Listen again. Are the sentences true (T) or false (F)?

1 *Macarena* was Fran's first CD. ☐
2 The singers were from Rio. ☐
3 Helder's first mobile phone was a Nokia. ☐
4 It was a small mobile phone. ☐
5 Don's first foreign holiday was last year. ☐
6 Fran's first film was *Jaws 3*. ☐

9 Write the rules to the game *I remember my first ...*

1 *Throw the dice.*

Speaking

10 Work in groups of three. Play *I remember my first ... .* Use the How to... box to help you.

How to... take part in a game

Take a go	A: *Is it my go?*
	B: *Yes, it's your go. Roll the dice.*
Losing	A: *Oh no! Not again!*
	B: *Bad luck! Never mind.*
Winning	A: *Yes! I win.*
	B: *Well done! That was great.*

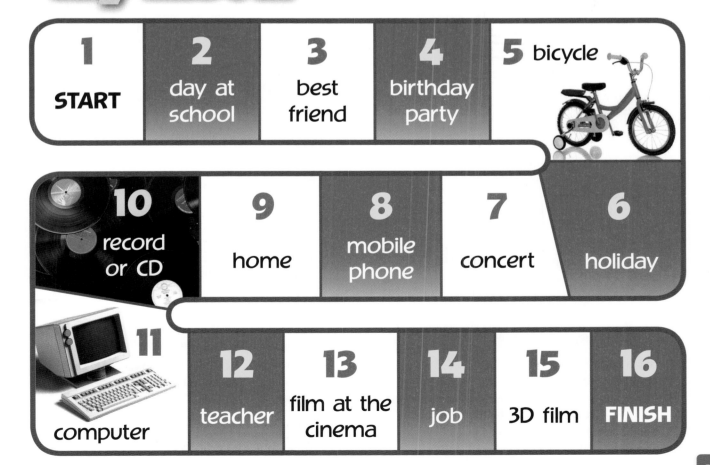

I remember my first ...

| 1 START | 2 day at school | 3 best friend | 4 birthday party | 5 bicycle |

| 10 record or CD | 9 home | 8 mobile phone | 7 concert | 6 holiday |

| 11 computer | 12 teacher | 13 film at the cinema | 14 job | 15 3D film | 16 FINISH |

Reading

1 **a** Complete the dialogues with words from the box.

> date   flight   holiday   trip   weekend

1

Woman: How was your _____ ?
Man: It wasn't very good. I was in bed all day on Saturday.
Woman: What was wrong with you?
Man: I don't know, but I'm OK now.

2

Girl 1: How was your _____ ?
Girl 2: It was great. He was nice, and funny and he was really tall.
Girl 1: How tall was he?
Girl 2: Almost two metres, I think.

3

Neighbour: How was your _____ ?
Mother: It was really nice. We were in Port Martin. There was no one on the beach, but it was quite far from the hotel.
Neighbour: How far was it?
Mother: About two kilometres.

4

Girl: Hi, Uncle Alan. How was your _____ ?
Uncle: It was OK, thanks, but it was quite long.
Girl: How long was it?
Uncle: About seven hours. And there weren't any free drinks!

5

Son: Oh, hi. How was your _____ ?
Father: It was nice.
Son: There was ... er ... a party here.
Father: How big was the party?
Son: About fifty people. One or two are still here.

b 🔊 2.37 Listen and check your answers.

2 Are the sentences true (T) or false (F)?

Dialogue 1	He was ill.	☐
Dialogue 2	Her date was good.	☐
Dialogue 3	Her holiday wasn't very good.	☐
Dialogue 4	His flight was very good.	☐
Dialogue 5	His parents were at home.	☐

3 Work in pairs. Choose a dialogue and practise it. Then act it out for the class.

Pronunciation | /aʊ/

4 **a** 🔊 2.38 Listen and repeat the words.

/aʊ/ how now wow house mouse

b Underline the /aʊ/ sounds and say the sentences.

1 Wow! How big is that mouse?
2 Now, how far is the nearest town?
3 Do you want to have a shower at my house?

c 🔊 2.39 Listen and check. Then repeat the sentences.

5 **a** Read the How to... box. Then ask your partner about his/her weekend.

How to... ask about a past experience

How was your day/weekend/trip/flight/ holiday/party/date?

☺ *It was nice/great/brilliant/fantastic.*

😐 *It was OK/alright.*
It wasn't bad.

☹ *It wasn't very good.*
It was awful/terrible/really bad.

---

b Work in pairs. Make up dialogues starting with these questions.

1 How was your day?
2 How was your trip?
3 How was your party?

A: *How was your day?*
B: *It was awful. I was late for work.*

Vocabulary | more adjectives

6 Complete the sentences with the adjectives in the box.

deep   far   heavy   long   tall   wide

1 This river is quite _____ . It's about 200 metres from one side to the other.
2 This road is very _____ . It's over 500 kilometres.
3 Her house is quite _____ away. It's five kilometres from here.
4 That building is very _____ . It's got thirty floors.
5 The swimming pool isn't very _____ . Be careful when you jump in.
6 My suitcase was really _____ . It was twenty-five kilos.

Grammar | Questions with *how*

7 **a** Underline the questions with *How* + adjective in the dialogues in exercise 1a.

b Complete the Active grammar box with adjectives from exercise 6.

Active grammar

How wide is the table?	It's about a metre wide.
How _____ was your journey?	About seven hours.
How _____ is that building?	It's thirty storeys _____ .
How _____ was the hotel from the town?	It was about twenty kilometres from the town.
How _____ is the water in the pool?	It's about two metres _____ .
How _____ were your bags?	They were very, very _____ .

---

see Reference page 87

8 Write a question for each sentence.

1 The room is ten metres wide.
How wide is the room?
2 The flight is about four hours.
3 He's one metre 85 centimetres tall.
4 The restaurant is 800 metres from here.
5 That building is twelve storeys tall.
6 The table is 3.5 metres long.

9 **a** Work in pairs. Ask and answer questions. Check your answers on page 119.

1 long/the River Thames
A: *How long is the River Thames?*
B: *It's 346 kilometres long.*
2 tall/the Eiffel Tower
3 far/Perth to nearest big city
4 long/the flight from New York to Madrid
5 deep/the Mediterranean, on average
6 heavy/a sixty kilogram person on the moon

b Work in pairs. Write more general knowledge questions. Then ask another pair.

Speaking

10 **a** Think about your last weekend away/holiday/flight/ birthday party. Write four adjectives to describe it.

b Work in pairs. Ask and answer questions.

A: *How was your last weekend away?*
B: *It was great. It was quite short.*
A: *How short was it?*

Can do | ask and answer simple questions about your childhood

1 **a** Who is your favourite writer?

b Read about Kagiso Otto and answer the questions.

1 Where is she from?

2 Who are her favourite authors?

2 Read the text again. Complete 1–4 with questions a–d.

a Were you happy?

b What were you good at?

c When you were a child, what were your hobbies?

d How bad?

3 **a** Look at the Lifelong learning box. Read the tip and answer the question.

Lifelong learning

Guess the meaning

! When you find a word that you don't know, try to guess the meaning.

e.g. *I was **into** reading.*

When you are *into* something, do you
a) like it or b) not like it?

b Read the text again and guess the meaning of words you don't know.

4 **a** Work in pairs. Write more questions to ask someone about their childhood.

b Interview a new partner. Use your questions from exercise 4a and the questions in the interview with Kagiso.

c Tell the class about your partner.

Pavel was born in Prague in 1979. He loves Prague and lives there now.

Fact file: Kagiso Otto

Born: in Cape Town, South Africa in 1955

Job: Writer

Books: *How Wide is the Valley* (1997), *It Was Twenty Years Ago* (2005)

Adam Applegate talks to Kagiso Otto about her childhood and her new book.

1 _____
I was into clothes and fashion. I still buy *Vogue* every month.

What else were you into?
I was into reading. My favourite authors were Wole Soyinka and Nadine Gordimer. They're still my favourite authors now.

2 _____
At school I was good at sport and English, but I was really bad at science.

3 _____
Really, really bad! My test scores were terrible.

Who was your favourite teacher?
My favourite teacher was Mr Selassie, my English teacher. He was fantastic.

4 _____
When I was a child, I was very happy. When I was a teenager, I wasn't very confident, so I wasn't happy.

Are you happy now?
I'm a writer, so I'm happy when I write. I love writing.

What is your new book about?
It's about life in South Africa in the 1970s. It's called *You Were My First Love.*

Past Simple of *to be*

Positive and negative

I	was wasn't (was not)	
You	were weren't (were not)	a good friend. born in 1980. late for class.
He She It	was wasn't	
You (plural) We They	were weren't	good friends. born in 1980. late for class.

Questions

Was	I	
Were	you	a happy teenager?
Was	he she it	at home last night? born in 1980?
Were	you we they	happy teenagers? at home last night? born in 1980?

Yes, I/he/she/it was.
No, I/he/she/it wasn't.
Yes, you/we/they were.
No, you/we/they weren't.

Wh- questions

Who was your first love?
Who was your favourite teacher?
What was your first CD?
What was your best holiday?
Where were you born?
Where was your sister yesterday?
When was your first film at the cinema?
When were you first in love?

Questions with *how*

How + noun
How was **your weekend**?
How was **your party**?
How was **your job interview**?

How + adjective
How long was your journey? (time)
How long/wide is the river? (distance)
How tall is she? (height)
How far is the hotel? (distance)
How heavy is your rucksack? (weight)
How deep is the swimming pool? (depth)

Key vocabulary

Saying years
1656 = sixteen fifty-six
1951 = nineteen fifty-one
2001 = two thousand and one
2012 = two thousand and twelve

Jobs
actor
artist
business person
dancer
leader
musician
politician
scientist
singer
sports star
writer

Past time expressions
yesterday
last night
yesterday morning/afternoon/evening
two days/six months/ten years ago
last week/month/year
in 1980/in 2010

Adjectives
deep
far
heavy
long
tall
wide

Listen to the explanations and vocabulary.
ACTIVEBOOK

see Writing bank page 127

1 Complete the text with *was* or *were* and guess the famous person.

Who am I?

I am a singer with a very famous band. I (1) *was* born on 26th July 1943, in the UK. My father and my grandfather (2) _____ teachers. My mother (3) _____ from Kent, in England. I (4) _____ a student at the London School of Economics – but only for two years. Bianca Pérez-Mora de Macias and Jerry Hall (5) _____ my wives. *Paint it Black* and *Satisfaction* (6) _____ two of my band's famous songs.

2 Write sentences with *wasn't/was* or *weren't/were*.

1 Sally/late/early

   Sally wasn't late. She was early.

2 My parents/at home/in a restaurant

   _____

3 I/at the theatre/at the cinema

   _____

4 Ian/born in 1981/born in 1979

   _____

5 It/a good film/very boring

   _____

6 We/rich/quite poor

   _____

7 You/my best friend/a good friend

   _____

8 Kerry and Mark/in Bogotà/in Cali

   _____

3 Complete the dialogue with *was*, *wasn't*, *were* or *weren't*.

A: (1) *Were* you at work last week?

B: No, I (2) _____ .

A: (3) _____ you on holiday?

B: Yes, I (4) _____ . I (5) _____ on holiday with Emily. We (6) _____ at her parents' house in the south of France.

A: (7) _____ it nice?

B: It (8) _____ beautiful! Her parents (9) _____ there, so we (10) _____ alone.

4 Put the words in the correct order to make questions. Then match the questions with the answers (a–e).

1 born? When you were

   When were you born? = c

2 was Who manager? your

   _____ = _____

3 school? your Where was

   _____ = _____

4 first What your job? was

   _____ = _____

5 weekend? your was How

   _____ = _____

a I was a call centre worker.

b It was great, thanks.

c In 1966.

d Her name was Ms Dickson.

e It was on Peak Street, opposite the hospital.

5 Complete the questions with *How* and an adjective from the box.

~~far~~   long   tall   wide

1 '*How far* is your flat from here?'
   'It's two kilometres away.'

2 '_____ is that film?'
   'It's two hours.'

3 '_____ is your living room?'
   'It's five metres from the door to the window.'

4 '_____ is your husband?'
   'He's one metre seventy centimetres.'

6 Write the jobs.

1 art – *artist*

2 singing – *singer*

3 dancing – _____

4 sport – _____

5 music – _____

6 science – _____

7 politics – _____

8 writing – _____

7 Complete the sentences with *ago*, *yesterday*, *in* or *last*.

1 Were you at home *yesterday* evening?

2 I wasn't in class two days _____ .

3 Were they married _____ 2005?

4 She was on holiday _____ week.

5 I was still in bed at nine o'clock _____ morning.

6 He was a teacher ten years _____ .

7 Where were you _____ night?

Lead-in

1 **a** Match the descriptions with the photos.

1 She spends a lot of money on clothes. She buys them online and pays by credit card. ☐
2 She invests in shares. She earns a lot of money. ☐
3 He sells fruit. He saves some money every month. ☐
4 He borrows money from the bank. The bank lends him money. He plays the lottery, but he never wins any money. ☐

b 🔵 2.40 Listen and check your answers.

2 **a** Complete the sentences with words from the box.

> borrow   buy   earn   in*vest*   lend   pay   save   sell   ~~spend~~   win

1 I *spend* a lot of money on clothes every month.
2 I sometimes _____ money from friends.
3 I never _____ money to friends.
4 I want to _____ my money in shares.
5 I try to _____ some money every month in the bank.
6 I never _____ by credit card.
7 I sometimes _____ things online.
8 I usually _____ my old things online.
9 I don't play the lottery, so I never _____ money on it.
10 I want to _____ €200 a day.

b Work in pairs. Ask and answer questions with *Do you (ever/usually) ...?*

A: *Do you spend a lot of money on clothes?*
B: *No, I don't. Do you?*

9.1 | Teenage jobs

Vocabulary | teenagers and money

1 a Match the phrases in the box with the pictures.

> clean and tidy at home ☐
> deliver newspapers ☐
> help your brother/sister with his/her homework ☐
> look after your neighbour's children ☐
> stack shelves ☐ wash cars ☐
> work nights in a factory ☐
> work part-time in a cinema ☐

b 🔊 2.41 Listen and check your answers. Then repeat the phrases.

2 How do teenagers earn money in your country?

A lot of teenagers work for their parents. Some of them have part-time jobs.

Listening

3 a 🔊 2.42 Listen to a radio programme and match phrases from exercise 1a to a person.

a Nicole Kidman
b Tom Cruise
c Amrik
d Lidia
e Eva

a Nicole Kidman = work part-time in a cinema

b Listen again. What job does each person do now? What was their worst teenage job?

	Job now	Worst job
Amrik		
Lidia		
Eva		
Eva's mother		

Grammar | Past Simple: regular verbs, positive

4 **a** Read the sentences from the radio programme. Underline the verbs in the Past Simple.

1 I washed cars in a car wash.
2 I finished work at seven in the evening.
3 She worked nights in a factory.
4 They started a restaurant.

b Complete the Active grammar box with the Past Simple of the verbs in brackets.

> ### Active grammar
>
> *I stayed for two years. (stay)*
> *You _____ after their children. (look)*
> *He/She/It _____ newspapers. (deliver)*
> *You _____ next door to a young couple. (live)*
> *We _____ the floor. (clean)*
> *They _____ four zloty an hour. (earn)*

see Reference page 97

5 Write the sentences in the Past Simple.

1 Josh likes the film.
Josh liked the film.
2 I help her brother with his homework.
3 We live in Manhattan.
4 They work nights in a factory.
5 I save some money every month.

6 Complete the text with the verbs from the box in the Past Simple.

> hate   listen   live   need   park   start   surf   wash   work

66 When my father was a teenager, he (1) _____ in a camper van for a while. He (2) _____ the van next to the beach. There were no showers so every morning he (3) _____ in the sea. He (4) _____ to music and (5) _____ a lot on a big, wooden surfboard. He was a waiter in a fast food restaurant. He (6) _____ it, but he (7) _____ the money. My mother (8) _____ in the same restaurant. That's how they (9) _____ going out. **99**

Pronunciation |

Past Simple *-ed* endings

7 **a** 🔊 2.43 Listen and repeat the Past Simple verbs.

/t/   liked   cooked   finished
/d/   cleaned   earned   lived
/ɪd/   hated   needed

b 🔊 2.44 Listen. Which sound do you hear at the end of the verbs – /t/, /d/ or /ɪd/?

1 I listened to music.
2 They worked in a shop.
3 We watched TV.
4 She loved that job.
5 I texted him.

c Listen again and check your answers. Then repeat the sentences.

8 Read the Lifelong learning box.

> ### Learn past forms
>
> **!** When you learn a new verb note the Simple Past tense and its pronunciation in your vocabulary notebook.
>
> ***deliver** (past = deliver**ed**) = take something to a place or person*
> /d/
> *I delivered pizzas on a scooter when I was a teenager.*

Lifelong learning

Writing

9 How did you earn money when you were younger? Write a paragraph using the prompts to help you.

When I was ... I worked in a ... .
I started at ... and I finished at ... .
I earned ... .
I liked ... , but I hated ... .

Vocabulary | money adjectives

1 **a** Match the words with the pictures.

> broke ☐ careful with money ☐
> careless with money ☐ generous ☐
> mean ☐ poor ☐ rich ☐

b 🔊 2.45 Listen and check your answers.

2 **a** Use the words and phrases in exercise 1a to make sentences about your family and friends.

My uncle is really generous. He always buys me a present when he goes on holiday.

b Work in pairs. Tell your partner about your friends and family.

Who wants to be a millionaire?

Curt Degerman from Sweden wasn't an average man. He didn't work and he didn't change his clothes very often. He walked the streets all day and collected tin cans from bins. In 2008 Curt died. His family checked his bank account. They were very surprised. Curt wasn't poor, he was rich. He was almost a millionaire! There was £731,000 in his bank account and another £250,000 in gold bars. How did Curt become so rich? Did he play the lottery and win? No, he didn't. Curt didn't earn a lot of money, but he earned a few pennies every day from collecting tin cans. He was very careful with this money. He didn't spend it, he invested it in shares. Curt looked at the business newspapers every day and his shares were successful. That's how he became a millionaire – almost!

Reading

3 **a** Look at the picture of Curt Degerman. Make guesses about him using the words in exercise 1a.

I think he is poor. I don't think he is ...

b Read the text. Were your guesses correct?

4 Read the text again. Are the sentences true (T) or false (F)? Correct the false sentences.

1 Curt lived a normal life. ☐
2 He died twenty years ago. ☐
3 Curt was a millionaire. ☐
4 Curt collected tin cans every day. ☐
5 Curt was rich because he played the lottery. ☐

5 Work in pairs. Do you think this is a happy story or a sad story? Give reasons.

Grammar | Past Simple: negatives and questions

6 Read the sentences from the text. Then complete the Active grammar box with *did* or *didn't*.

1 He didn't work and he didn't change his clothes.
2 Did he play the lottery and win?
3 He didn't earn a lot of money.
4 How did Curt become so rich?

Active grammar

Negative

I didn't call.

He _____ earn a lot of money.

They _____ play the lottery.

Yes/No questions

_____ you invest the money?

_____ she want to be an actor?

_____ they check his bank account?

   Yes, I/he/she/they _____ .

   No, I/he/she/they _____ .

Wh- questions

How much money _____ he earn?

Where _____ you live?

---

see Reference page 97

7 Complete the dialogues with the Past Simple form of the verbs given.

1 *enjoy*
   A: _____ you _____ your first day at work?
   B: No, I _____ . It was terrible.

2 *live*
   A: Where _____ you _____ when you were a teenager? Australia?
   B: No, I _____ _____ in Australia. I lived in New Zealand.

3 *borrow*
   A: I _____ _____ any money from Dad. _____ you _____ any money from him?
   B: No, I _____ , but Sam _____ some.

4 *watch*
   A: _____ you _____ that TV programme about money?
   B: No, I _____ . I _____ _____ TV last night.

5 *start*
   A: What time _____ you _____ work?
   B: Half past nine. I _____ a bit late.

Pronunciation | /ɔ:/ and /ɪ:/

8 2.46 Listen and repeat the words.

/ɔ:/ poor four more sure your
/ɪ:/ mean clean three she street

9 **a** Underline the /ɔ:/ sounds and circle the /ɪ:/ sounds in the sentences. Then say the sentences.

1 She's not poor, she's mean.
2 Is he forty-three or forty-four? I'm sure he's forty-four.
3 Shall we take a tour now? I want to see the city before we leave.

b 2.47 Listen and check your answers. Then repeat the sentences.

Speaking

10 **a** Look at the photos and use the prompts to make questions about Vaughan Bailey and Anya Peters.

Vaughan Bailey

1 Why/live on the streets?
2 What sport/play?
3 Why/change his job?
4 What/his new job?
5 What competition/enter?
6 What/his job now?

Anya Peters

1 Why/need a new job?
2 Where/start living?
3 Where/shower and wash her clothes?
4 she/like her new life?
5 What/do in the library?
6 How/Anya's life now?

b Can you guess any of the answers?

11 **a** Work in pairs.

Student A: read about Vaughan on page 118.

Student B: read about Anya on page 114.

b Tell your partner about Vaughan/Anya.

Vaughan's parents divorced when he was sixteen. He lived ...

c Ask more questions about your partner's text. Use the prompts in exercise 10a.

9.3 | A woman in a man's world

Grammar	Past Simple: irregular verbs
Can do	make simple statements about money habits

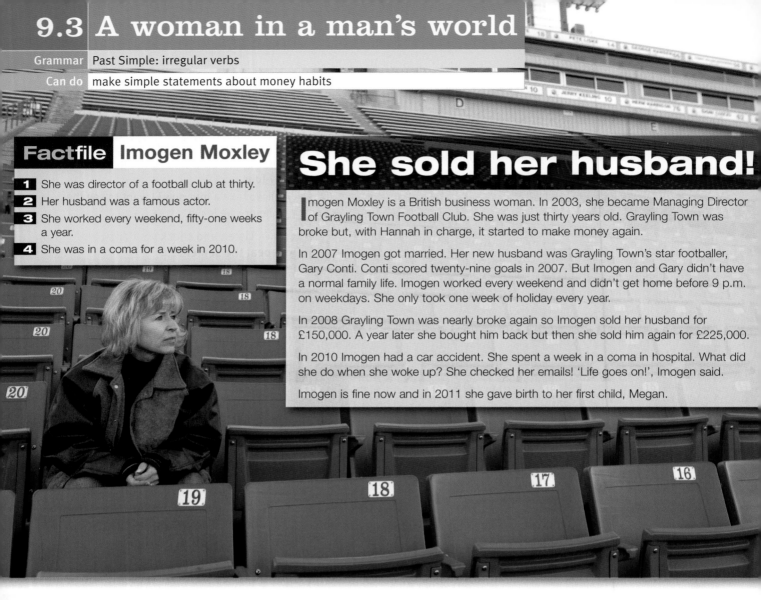

Factfile | Imogen Moxley

1 She was director of a football club at thirty.

2 Her husband was a famous actor.

3 She worked every weekend, fifty-one weeks a year.

4 She was in a coma for a week in 2010.

She sold her husband!

Imogen Moxley is a British business woman. In 2003, she became Managing Director of Grayling Town Football Club. She was just thirty years old. Grayling Town was broke but, with Hannah in charge, it started to make money again.

In 2007 Imogen got married. Her new husband was Grayling Town's star footballer, Gary Conti. Conti scored twenty-nine goals in 2007. But Imogen and Gary didn't have a normal family life. Imogen worked every weekend and didn't get home before 9 p.m. on weekdays. She only took one week of holiday every year.

In 2008 Grayling Town was nearly broke again so Imogen sold her husband for £150,000. A year later she bought him back but then she sold him again for £225,000.

In 2010 Imogen had a car accident. She spent a week in a coma in hospital. What did she do when she woke up? She checked her emails! 'Life goes on!', Imogen said.

Imogen is fine now and in 2011 she gave birth to her first child, Megan.

Reading

1 Read the fact file about Imogen Moxley. Don't read the article yet. Guess which sentence is <u>not</u> true.

2 **a** Read the text about Imogen Moxley and check your answer.

b Read the text again and answer the questions.

1 When did Imogen become Managing Director of Grayling Town Football Club?
2 What was Grayling Town's problem?
3 When did Imogen get married?
4 How much did she sell her husband for in 2008?
5 Why was Imogen in hospital in 2010?
6 What did she do when she was awake again?
7 What did Imogen do in 2011?

3 Work in pairs. Do you admire Imogen Moxley? Why/Why not?

I admire her because she's successful in the world of football. I think ...

Vocabulary | high numbers

4 **a** 🔊 2.48 Listen and repeat the high numbers.

750	seven hundred and fifty
999	nine hundred and ninety-nine
1,000	one thousand
2,500	two thousand five hundred
6,520	six thousand, five hundred and twenty
10,010	ten thousand and ten
300,502	three hundred thousand, five hundred and two
1,000,000	a/one million

b Work in pairs.

Student A: write two high numbers, then say them.

Student B: write the numbers.

5 🔊 2.49 Listen. Write the dates and prices you hear.

Date	Footballer	Price
1928	David Jack	£10,890
	Omar Sivori	
	Johann Cryuff	
	Guiseppe Savoldi	
	Luis Figo	
	Cristiano Ronaldo	

Grammar | Past Simple: irregular verbs

6 **a** Read the text again and <u>underline</u> all the verbs in the Past Simple.

b Complete the Active grammar box with the Past Simple form of the verbs.

c 🔊 2.50 Listen and check your answers.

Active grammar

become	became	go	went
buy	_____	have	had
do	did	sell	_____
find	found	spend	_____
get	_____	take	_____
give	_____		

see Reference page 97

7 **a** Work in pairs. Say a verb. Your partner says the Past Simple form.

A: *have*   B: *had*

b Correct the mistakes.

1 My father gived me his old car.
My father gave me his old car.
2 Did you bought a new phone?
3 I becomed class president at school in 2001.
4 When I was younger, I didn't had a bike.
5 Why did you tooked my wallet?
6 She didn't did her homework.
7 After the film we goed out for dinner.
8 Did you spent all your money?

8 Rewrite the paragraph using the Past Simple.

"I get up early on Saturdays. I take my daughter to swimming club. Then I go home and I do some exercise. I have lunch around one o'clock. In the afternoon I go shopping with my family. My daughter buys new clothes. I don't buy anything. I'm careful with my money. I don't spend a lot."

I got up early last Saturday. I took my daughter ...

9 What did you do last weekend? Tell your partner.

Listening

10 **a** 🔊 2.51 Read the questionnaire then listen and put the questions in the order you hear them.

Money questionnaire

☐ **A** Do you always give big tips?
1 always
2 sometimes
3 never

☐ **B** Are you a saver or a spender?
1 a saver
2 a bit of both
3 a spender

☐ **C** What financial advice do you give to young people?
I tell them to ...
1 work hard
2 have fun
3 start a family

☐ **D** Were your parents careful with money?
1 yes
2 one was and one wasn't
3 no

☐ **E** How do you usually pay for things?
1 by cash
2 by credit card
3 by cheque

b Listen again. What were Imogen's answers?

Speaking

11 **a** Work in pairs. Add three more questions to the questionnaire in exercise 10a.

b Read the How to... box.

How to... talk about questionnaire results

Everyone/Everybody usually pays by cash.
Most people are savers, not spenders.
Some people usually pay by credit card.
No one/Nobody gives big tips.

c Guess the questionnaire answers for most people in your class.

I think most people usually pay by credit card.

12 Ask the questions to the students in your class. Were your guesses correct?

The Internet Millionaire Game
Make the right decisions and make a million!

Rules

Your aim is to make £1,000,000.
Work in pairs. Start at 1. Read the card and
make a decision together. Continue like this.
Try to make the right decisions. Too many
wrong decisions and you lose all your money!

CARD 1

You have a part-time job in a
supermarket. You stack shelves.
In the evening you surf the
Internet and design websites. You
want to be an Internet millionaire!
Last year you designed a website
for your rich uncle. You earned
£10,000.
What do you want to do?
• I want to start a business.
  (Go to 6 on page 111)
• I want to invest the money in
  shares. (Go to 10 on page 113)

CARD 2

You invested the rest
of your money. You
bought shares in a small
company. The company
wasn't successful and you
lost all your money.
In English there is a
saying: 'Don't put all your
eggs in one basket'. The
game is over for you.

CARD 3

You decided to do market research.
That was a good decision. The
research was expensive, but it was
very useful. You learnt that people
want 'apps' for their mobile phones.
What do you want to do?
• I want to go to night school and
  learn to write apps.
  (Go to 17 on page 114)
• I don't want to go to night school.
  I want to design websites.
  (Go to 21 on page 115)

CARD 4

You made the right decision. You
said no to the supermarket. You
didn't earn the money but you also
didn't become ill from stress.
Last year you hired two new website
designers. Your business earned
over £1,000,000. You are now an
Internet millionaire! Congratulations!

CARD 5

You continued with your business,
but now you need more money.
What do you want to do?
• I want to borrow £50,000 from the
  bank. (Go to 15 on page 114)
• I don't want to borrow any money.
  (Go to 18 on page 115)

1   Can you name any Internet millionaires or billionaires?

2   **a**   Read the rules for *The Internet Millionaire Game*.

    b   Play *The Internet Millionaire Game* with your
partner. Can you make a million?

A: *What do you want to do? Shall we invest the
money or shall we start a business?*

B: *I don't know. What do you want to do?*

A: *Let's start a business.*

B: *OK. Let's do that.*

3   Find a new partner. Tell him/her what you did in the
game.

    We started a business. Then we borrowed £50,000 ...

9 Reference

Past Simple: regular verbs

Positive and negative

I	lived	
You	didn't live	in Rome.
He/She/It	worked	in a nice hotel.
You	didn't work	with my sister.
We	stayed	here for two years.
They	didn't stay	

Past Simple: irregular verbs

Positive and negative

I	bought	
You	didn't buy	a nice laptop.
He/She/It	found	a cat.
You	didn't find	some chocolate.
We	had	a phone.
They	didn't have	

A lot of verbs are irregular in the Past Simple, for example:

become – became
buy – bought
come – came
do – did
eat – ate
find – found
get – got
give – gave
go – went
have – had
make – made
read /riːd/ – read /red/
say – said
see – saw
sell – sold
speak – spoke
spend – spent
win – won
write – wrote

See the Irregular verbs list on page 133.

Past Simple: questions

Yes/No questions

We use the infinitive form of the verb in questions.
~~Did they moved to Paris?~~ Did they **move** to Paris?
~~Did she bought a flat?~~ Did she **buy** a flat?
Did you **find** your bag?
    Yes, I did.   No, I didn't.
Did she **live** in Rome when she was young?
    Yes, she did.   No, she didn't.
Did we **buy** them a present?
    Yes, we did.   No, we didn't.
Did they **stay** in a hotel?
    Yes, they did.   No, they didn't.

Wh- questions

When did she **become** Managing Director?
How did he **become** so rich?
What time did you **start** work?
Who did you **talk** to?

Key vocabulary

Money verbs
borrow buy earn invest lend pay save sell
spend win

Teenagers and money
clean and tidy at home   deliver newspapers
help your brother/sister with his/her homework
look after your neighbour's children   stack shelves
wash cars   work nights in a factory
work part-time in a cinema

Money adjectives
broke   careful with money   careless with money
generous   mean   poor   rich

High numbers

800	eight hundred
850	eight hundred and fifty
999	nine hundred and ninety-nine
1,001	one thousand and one
1,500	one thousand, five hundred
4,810	four thousand, eight hundred and ten
20,005	twenty thousand and five
200,113	two hundred thousand, one hundred and thirteen
1,000,000	a/one million
20,000,000	twenty million

Listen to the explanations and vocabulary.
ACTIVEBOOK

see Writing bank page 128

9 Review and practice

1 Complete the email with the verbs in the box in the Past Simple.

> clean   cook   play   ~~stay~~   wash   watch

Hi Felicia

How was your weekend? I (1) _stayed_ in bed all morning on Saturday! It was fantastic. In the evening my friend Carlos (2) _____ dinner for me and we (3) _____ a film. That was nice! On Sunday morning I (4) _____ tennis with my friend Anita. In the afternoon I (5) _____ the house and (6) _____ the car. That wasn't very exciting.

Hope you're OK. Send me an email soon.

Kiera

2 Complete the crossword with the Past Simple form of the verbs.

Down

1 make
3 spend
4 lend
5 buy
6 win

Across

2 give
3 sell
5 become
7 take
8 find
9 get

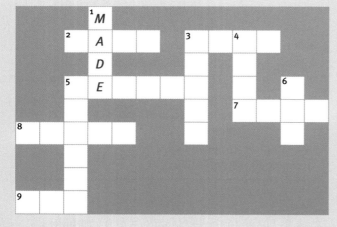

3 Complete the dialogues with the verbs in brackets in the Past Simple.

A: Rox and Yanni (1) _went_ (go) on holiday last week.
B: Again! (2) _____ they _____ (win) a lot of money?
A: No, they didn't. Yanni (3) _____ (invest) some money in shares last year and they (4) _____ (do) very well. He (5) _____ (buy) a new car, too.
B: Is the money all gone now?
A: I think so. He (6) _____ _____ (not save) any.

C: What jobs (7) _____ you _____ (do) when you were a teenager? (8) _____ you _____ your dad's car? (wash)
D: Yes, I did. But I (9) _____ _____ (not get) any money for it.
C: (10) _____ you _____ (help) your brother with his homework, too?
D: No, I didn't. But I (11) _____ (look) after my neighbour's children.
C: I (12) _____ _____ (not do) that. My neighbours (13) _____ _____ (not have) any children. I (14) _____ (work) in a supermarket. I (15) _____ _____ (not stack) shelves. I just (16) _____ (clean) the floor.

4 Complete the dialogues with a word that has the same meaning as the expression in **bold**.

1 A: I used the money to **buy shares**.
   B: Oh, you _invested_ the money.
2 A: I **haven't got any money**.
   B: Oh, you're _____ .
3 A: I **put the money in the bank**.
   B: Oh, you _____ the money.
4 A: I **used all the money** to buy things.
   B: Oh, you _____ the money.
5 A: I **think before I spend** money.
   B: Oh, you're _____ _____ money.
6 A: I **get** $100 a day from my work.
   B: Oh, you _____ $100 a day.
7 A: I don't work in the day. **I work at night**.
   B: Oh, you _____ _____ .
8 A: I **put boxes on shelves in a supermarket**.
   B: Oh, you _____ _____ .

5 Write the numbers in words.

1 1,438
   one thousand, four hundred and thirty-eight
2 651
3 15,300
4 39,421
5 121,890
6 2,750,480

Lead-in

1 Match four of the phrases in the box with the photos.

> change jobs ~~fall in love~~ get a job get fit get married
> go to university graduate have a baby learn to drive
> leave home meet someone special move quit your job
> re<u>tire</u> start your own business

2 **a** Put the phrases in exercise 1 into the correct group.

1 Love and family: _fall in love_, _____ , _____ , _____
2 House: _____ , _____
3 Personal: _____ , _____
4 School/University: _____ , _____
5 Work: _____ , _____ , _____ , _____ , _____

b 🔊 2.52 Listen and check your answers.

3 🔊 2.53 Listen. Two people talk about their life changes. Answer true (T) or false (F).

Woman		**Man**	
1 She quit her job as a teacher. ☐		5 He left home at eighteen. ☐	
2 She went to university. ☐		6 He lived alone for five years. ☐	
3 She got a job in a school. ☐		7 He met someone special. ☐	
4 She likes her job. ☐		8 He got married last year. ☐	

4 **a** Work with a partner and talk about your life changes. Say when they happened.

I changed jobs last year.

b What do you want to do in the future? Tell your partner.

I want to learn to drive. I don't want to start my own business.

Grammar	*going to*: positive
Can do	talk about your future plans

Reading

1 Which country in the world do you want to visit most? How long do you want to stay?

2 **a** Read the messages and put them in order.

b Work in pairs. Compare your answers to exercise 2a. How did you decide on the order?

A ☐

Rosa Jansen

Wall **Info** **Photos**

What's on your mind?

Attach .... **Share**

Rosa I met some great people last week. They're going to drive to Wellington tomorrow and then go to the South Island! I think I'm going to go with them :)
· Tuesday 2:39 p.m. · Like · Comment

Comment
Callum It sounds great. Call me soon xx

B ☐

From: rosajansen@saymail.net
To: callumkelly@qst_media.com
Subject: First day in New Zealand!

Dear Callum,

How are you? It's my first day here in New Zealand and guess what? The airline lost my luggage! I'm at a hostel now and everyone is really friendly, so don't worry. I can borrow some clothes.

I miss you already. It's only for three months and then we're going to be together again. I can't wait!

Rosa xxx

C ☐
Hello Callum,
How are you? I don't know how to say this, but …

D ☐
I'm at the airport. I've got my passport. I'm scared! I'm going to call you every day. Wait for me! xxxx

E ☐

From: rosaJansen@saymail.net
To: callumkelly@qst_media.com
Subject: A couple more weeks

Hi Callum,
Wow! Three months goes really quickly. I'm in Queenstown in the South Island and I really love it here. I really miss you, but I want to stay a couple of weeks longer. Some friends and I are going to fly to Australia on Wednesday. Yes, Australia! We're going to see Ayers Rock and the Great Barrier Reef! Then we're going to go to Sydney! Daniel, one of my friends here, is going to lend me some money to buy the ticket.

I must go – we're going to go sightseeing in a minute.

Love you,

Rosa x

PS How are you?

F ☐
Thanx 4 emails. Sorry, really busy. Going to stay a bit longer in Sydney. Just got work visa and job in café here. Call you soon! Rosa x
PS lost my phone – this from Daniel's phone

3 Read the messages again. Are the sentences true (T) or false (F)? Correct the false sentences.

1   Rosa lost her bags in the hostel. ☐
2   At the beginning of her trip, Rosa missed Callum. ☐
3   Rosa decided to fly to Wellington. ☐
4   After three months Rosa wanted to go home. ☐
5   Rosa went to Sydney with Daniel. ☐

4 Look at the Lifelong learning box. Read the tip and answer the question.

> ### Learning phrases
>
> There are a lot of useful phrases in English. Make a note when you read them or hear them. Try to use the ones you like when you speak.
>
> **Guess what!** *I'm going to quit my job.*
> **I can't wait!** *It's going to be fantastic.*
>
> What other useful phrases can you find in the messages?

Lifelong learning

5 **a** Work in pairs. What do you think Rosa says in her last email? Write the email.

b What is your advice for Rosa? What is your advice for Callum?

Rosa – go back to Callum. He misses you a lot!

Grammar | *going to*: positive

6 **a** <u>Underline</u> all the examples of *going to* + verb in the messages.

b Complete the Active grammar box with the correct form of *going to*.

c 🔊 2.54 Listen and check your answers.

> ### Active grammar
>
> We use *going to* + verb to talk about future plans and intentions.
> *I'm going to go with them.*
> *You're going to wait for me.*
> *He _____ lend me some money.*
> *You're going to visit me next year.*
> *We _____ see Ayers Rock.*
> *They _____ drive to Wellington tomorrow.*
>
> We often use future time expressions with *going to*. For example:
> *tomorrow   next week/month/year   soon*

see Reference page 107

7 Complete the text with the correct form of *going to*.

The next three months

(1) I**'m going to get** (get) fit. It's March and I want to look good on the beach. My brother, Marik, (2) _____ (change) jobs. He's a waiter now but he (3) _____ (be) a cook. My two friends, Kasia and Diego, (4) _____ (start) their own business.

The next two years

I (5) _____ (learn) to drive and I (6) _____ (meet) someone special (I hope!) and fall in love. My parents (7) _____ (retire) and my dad (8) _____ (start) his own business. He's a manager but he wants to be an artist when he retires. My friend Per and I (9) _____ (take) a holiday to Tanzania. We (10) _____ (do) a safari.

The next ten years

I (11) _____ (get) married and have a baby. My sister Maryla (12) _____ (study) at university and graduate. She (13) _____ (meet) someone special and fall in love, too. My friends, Kasia and Diego, (14) _____ (be) rich.

Speaking

8 Work in pairs.

1   What are your plans for the next three months/two years/ten years?
2   What plans have your friends and family got?

10.2 Cheer up!

Grammar *going to*: negatives and questions

Can do ask and answer about personal plans

Vocabulary | emotions

1 **a** Look at the photos. How does each person feel, ☺ or ☹?

b Match the words in the box with the photos.

> angry ☐ bored ☐ depressed ☐
> excited ☐ happy ☐ nervous ☐
> scared ☐ tired ☐ upset ☐

c 🔘 2.55 Listen and check your answers.

2 **a** What do you do when you feel the emotions in exercise 1b? Write sentences.

When I'm bored, I watch TV.

When I'm happy, I listen to music.

b Work in pairs. Read your sentences out loud.

A: *When I'm nervous, I bite my nails.*

B: *Really? I don't. When I'm nervous, I talk a lot.*

Listening

3 **a** 🔘 2.56 Listen and match the dialogues with the emotions in exercise 1b.

Dialogue a = photo ____   Dialogue b = photo ____

b Listen again and answer the questions.

Dialogue a

1   What did Pippa do this morning? Why?
2   What's the problem now?
3   Is she going to tell her husband?

Dialogue b

4   Why isn't Omar happy?
5   How old are his children?
6   What is Sef going to do?

4 **a** 🔘 2.57 Listen to three extracts from the dialogues. Circle the phrases you hear in the How to... box.

> ### How to... say goodbye
>
> *Goodbye./Bye./See you.*
> *See you later/soon/tomorrow/on Monday.*
> *Have a nice weekend/evening/holiday!*

b Work in pairs. Say goodbye in these situations.

1   It's Wednesday evening.

A: *See you tomorrow!* B: *Yes, see you tomorrow.*

2   It's Friday evening.
3   Student B is going to go on holiday tomorrow.
4   You are going to meet again in an hour.

Grammar | *going to*: negatives and questions

5 **a** Read these sentences from the dialogues. Then complete the Active grammar box.

1   I'm not going to lie to him.
2   He isn't going to be happy.
3   They aren't going to live in another country.
4   'Are you going to tell him?' 'Yes, I am.'
5   What are you going to do?

b 🔘 2.58 Listen and check your answers.

> ### Active grammar
>
> ⊖ *I'm not going to borrow his phone again.*
> *He _____ going to like me.*
> *They _____ going to live at home.*
>
> ❓ *_____ you going to buy him a new one?*
> *Yes, I _____ .*
> *No, I _____ .*
> *_____ he going to be happy?*
> *Yes, he _____ .*
> *No, he _____ .*
> *_____ they going to go to university?*
> *Yes, they _____ .*
> *No, they _____ .*
> *What _____ you going to do?*
> *Where _____ they going to go?*

see Reference page 107

7 Work in pairs and write dialogues.

1 they're tired/go to bed early? // Yes

A: *They're tired.*

B: *Are they going to go to bed early?*

A: *Yes, they are.*

2 I'm bored/watch TV // No

3 she's angry/talk to him // Yes

4 he's depressed/go to the doctor // No

5 I'm excited/tell your parents // Yes

6 they're scared/call the police // No

Pronunciation | /ɡəʊɪŋ tə/

8 **a** ⊙ 2.59 Listen to the dialogues in exercise 7. How is *to* pronounced in *going to*?

b Work in pairs. Look at the audioscripts on page 143 and practise the dialogues.

Speaking

9 **a** Complete the questionnaire on page 111.

b Work in pairs. Compare your answers.

A: *Are you going to sing in the shower?*

B: *I already do that. Are you going to wear yellow clothes?*

A: *No, I'm not. It's a silly idea.*

c Tell the class about your partner.

Pierre already does regular exercise and he smiles a lot. He's going to go to bed early sometimes because it's a good idea. He isn't going to ...

6 Write complete questions and sentences with *going to*.

1 I/not retire/when I'm sixty-five.

I'm not going to retire when I'm sixty-five.

2 A: you/change jobs?

   B: Yes

A: *Are you going to change jobs?*

B: *Yes, I am.*

3 my sister/not leave home

4 A: your parents/move

   B: No

5 When/they/learn to drive?

6 What/you/do this weekend?

7 She/not come this evening

8 Our teacher/not give us any homework

9 How/you/get home?

10 A: Jon/get married?

    B: No

10.3 Giving gifts

Grammar *why* and *because*

Can do give and receive a present

Reading

1 Work in pairs. Ask and answer the questions.

1 What presents did you get on your last birthday?

2 Are any presents unlucky in your country?

3 Are any colours unlucky in your country?

I got an iPod from my husband on my last birthday.

2 a Work in pairs.

Student A: read the text on page 119. Then answer these questions.

1 How many flowers do people give in China?

2 What number is lucky in South Korea?

3 Are red roses a good present for a German friend?

4 What colours are lucky in India?

Student B: read the text on page 114. Then answer these questions.

1 What do Chinese people usually do when you give a gift?

2 When do people open a gift in Morocco?

3 When do Korean people get money as a gift?

4 What is a bad present for a man from Saudi Arabia?

b Close your books and tell your partner about your text.

In Japan people never give four things. It's unlucky ...

c Read your partner's questions above. Can you answer the questions?

3 What traditions are there for presents in your country?

In my country the bride and groom give presents to the guests at the end of a wedding.

4 What is important in your country when you give a present? Make rules for a foreigner.

Don't give scissors or knives. They are unlucky.

Grammar | *why* and *because*

5 a Read the text. Then complete the Active grammar box with *why* or *because*.

In the UK wedding guests usually give the bride and groom a present. But a new report says that 45% of brides don't want a present. They want money. We talked to two brides.

Why do you want money?

We want money because weddings are expensive and because we want to go on holiday after the wedding.
Debbie

Why do you want money?

Because we need to buy a new car. We don't need plates and bowls and things because we already have them.
Anita

Active grammar

We use *why* to ask for a reason.
We use *because* to give a reason.

_____ did you buy a DVD?
I bought a DVD _____ it's Adam's birthday.

_____ did you quit your job?
_____ I hated it and _____ I want to live abroad.

see Reference page 107

b 🔵 2.60 Listen and check your answers.

6 Use the prompts to write questions in the Past Simple with *why*. Then write an answer with *because*.

1 you wake up early // want/go for a swim

Why did you wake up early?

Because I wanted to go for a swim.

2 he buy that bike? // like it

3 you borrow €10? // want/buy some food

4 you give them a gift? // decide/say thank you

5 we move? // need a big house

6 she go to university? // want/study Art

Pronunciation | sentence stress

7 **a** 🔊 2.61 Listen and <u>underline</u> the stressed words.

1 <u>Why</u> do you <u>go</u> to the <u>gym</u>?
2 Why do you like your job?
3 I bought him a book because he wants to learn to read.
4 I went to the doctor because I needed some medicine.

b Listen again and repeat the rhythm and the sentences.

Vocabulary | presents

8 **a** Match the words and phrases in the box with the pictures.

beauty products ☐   chocolates ☐
a clock ☐   glasses ☐   jewellery ☐
a photo frame ☐   a plant ☐
plates and bowls ☐   tickets for a show ☐
a toy ☐   a vase ☐
a voucher for a shop ☐

b 🔊 2.62 Listen and check your answers. Then repeat the words and phrases.

9 **a** Which gifts are good for these situations?

1 a friend's birthday   3 a retirement
2 a cousin's wedding   4 dinner at a friend's house

I think flowers are a good gift for dinner at a friend's house.

b Choose a present for five people in the class. You can use the presents in exercise 8 or your own ideas. Then tell your partner and explain why you chose them.

A: *I gave Miriam some plates and bowls.*
B: *Why did you give her plates and bowls?*
A: *Because she's going to move to a new house soon. She's going to need them.*

10 **a** 🔊 2.63 Read and listen to the dialogue in the How to... box. Then repeat it.

How to... give and receive gifts

A: *This is for you.*
B: *Oh, thank you. That's really kind of you.*
A: *Don't mention it. / You're welcome.*

b Give the presents to the people in exercise 9b. Explain why you gave them.

A: *These are for you. They're two tickets for a show.*
B: *Oh, thank you. That's really kind of you.*
A: *You're welcome.*
B: *Why did you choose two tickets for a show?*
A: *Because you work a lot and you need to have fun.*

10 | Communication

1 **a** Look at the photos of different holidays. Put them in order for you (1 = favourite, 2 = second favourite, etc).

b Work in pairs. Compare your lists.

2 **a** Think about your favourite holiday from the past. Complete the notes about it.

66 My favourite holiday was in (year). I went to (place) with (person). We stayed there for (days/weeks). We stayed in a (hotel/B&B/etc). In the daytime we (activity) and in the evening we (activity). I felt really (emotion) on that holiday. **99**

b Work in pairs. Ask and answer questions about your favourite holiday.

A: *When was your favourite holiday?*

B: *It was in 2008.*

A: *Where did you go?*

3 Which countries/cities/places do you want to go to on holiday in the future? Tell your partner.

I want to go to the Great Barrier Reef in Australia and I want to go to Beijing in China.

4 **a** Work in pairs. You and your partner won a competition yesterday. You won your holiday of a lifetime. Read the rules below.

The Rules

1 It is a two-week holiday.
2 You can fly to three different places.
3 You always fly from west to east around the world.
4 You always travel together.

b Plan your holiday of a lifetime with your partner. Decide:

1 where (e.g. Marrakech in Morocco)
2 how long (e.g. four days)
3 your plans (e.g. go to the markets, see the Atlas Mountains)

A: *How about Rio in Brazil?*

B: *OK, good idea. How long are we going to stay there?*

5 Explain your holiday plans to the class.

First we're going to fly to Rio in Brazil. We're going to stay there for four days. We're going to relax on Ipanema Beach and ...

Going to

We use *going to* for future plans.

Positive

I'm You're He's/She's/It's You're We're They're	going to	change jobs. learn to drive. quit my job. go to university.

Negative

I'm not You aren't He/She/It isn't You aren't We aren't They aren't	going to	get married. leave home. move. graduate.

Yes/No questions

Are you going to quit your job?
    Yes, I am.
    No, I'm not.
Is she going to have a baby?
    Yes, she is.
    No, she isn't.
Are they going to get married?
    Yes, they are.
    No, they aren't.

Wh- questions

What are you going to do?
What's she going to buy?
Where are they going to live?
Where's she going to move to?
When are you going to see her?
When are they going to arrive?
Who's going to call him?
Who are you going to talk to?

Why and because

We use *why* to ask for a reason.
Why did you buy a new bicycle?
Why are you at home on Saturday evening?
Why are you going to move?

We use *because* to give reasons. You can join two clauses with *because*.
*I bought a new bicycle **because** I want to cycle to work.*
*I'm at home **because** I'm ill.*
*I'm going to move **because** I don't like my house.*

You can begin your answer with *because*.
Why are you so tired?
Because *I went to bed late.*

Key vocabulary

Life changes
change jobs
fall in love
get a job
get fit
get married
go to university
graduate
have a baby
learn to drive
leave home
meet someone special
move
quit your job
retire
start your own business

Emotions
angry bored depressed excited happy
nervous scared tired upset

Presents
beauty products chocolates a clock glasses
jewellery a photo frame a plant plates and bowls
tickets for a show a toy a vase
a voucher for a shop

 Listen to the explanations and vocabulary.
ACTIVEBOOK

 see Writing bank page 129

10 Review and practice

1 Complete the email with the correct form of *going to* and the verb in brackets.

My family and I (1) _are going to be_ (be) very busy next year. We (2) _____ (move). This house is really small. But we (3) _____ (move) far. We all like this area.

I (4) _____ (start) my own business. I don't like my job, but I (5) _____ (quit) now. We need the money.

My daughter Lillian (6) _____ (go) to university. She wanted to do Law, but she (7) _____ (do) that now. Her grades weren't very high. She (8) _____ (study) French.

My two sons, Mark and George, (9) _____ (leave) home. They (10) _____ (live) together. Mark (11) _____ (travel) abroad and George (12) _____ (live) with his friend. We (13) _____ (have) a busy year!

2 Write the question and answer in full. Use *going to*.

1 you/learn to swim? // ✗

A: *Are you going to learn to swim?*

B: *No, I'm not.*

2 she/help you with your homework? // ✓

_____

3 we/go on holiday this year? // ✗

_____

4 your children/leave home soon? // ✓

_____

5 you and your wife/have a party this year? // ✗

_____

6 you/get fit // ✓

_____

3 Write questions to find the missing information.

1 ____ is going to retire.

Who's going to retire?

2 I'm going to buy a ____ .

What are you going to buy?

3 They're going to go to ____ .

_____

4 We're going to see ____ at the cinema.

_____

5 ____ is going to get fit.

_____

6 I'm going to call ____ .

_____

7 Lucy's going to study ____ at university.

_____

8 Tom and Jo are going to buy a new house in ____ .

_____

4 Complete the sentences with the verbs in the box.

change fall get ~~learn~~ leave meet quit start

1 When are you going to _learn_ to drive?
2 Is your daughter going to _____ home?
3 Only fools _____ in love!
4 Are you happy or do you want to _____ jobs?
5 I really want to _____ my own business.
6 Do you think you're going to _____ someone special?
7 I want to _____ fit but, I hate the gym.
8 She wants to _____ her job. She doesn't like it.

5 Choose the correct words in *italics*.

1 A: You seem a bit *bored/happy/nervous*.
B: I've got an exam tomorrow. I hate exams.
2 A: You seem a bit *depressed/excited/angry*.
B: Yes, I hate my job and my wife doesn't love me.
3 A: You seem a bit *scared/tired/angry*.
B: I went to bed late last night.
4 A: You seem *happy/bored/depressed*.
B: I'm going to get married!
5 A: You seem *scared/excited/bored*.
B: There's nothing on TV. I don't know what to do.
6 A: Are you *upset/tired/excited*?
B: Yes. My cat died yesterday.
7 A: Why are you *happy/scared/angry*?
B: I think there's a stranger in my house.

6 Choose a present from the box for each person.

beauty products ~~a clock~~ jewellery plates and bowls tickets for a show a voucher

1 A: What shall we get Ella for her birthday?
B: Let's get her _a clock_. She never knows the time.
2 A: What shall we buy Pete for his birthday?
B: Let's buy him _____ for DVD World. He always buys all his films from there.
3 A: What shall we get for Jared?
B: Let's get him _____ . He loves the theatre and musicals.
4 A: What shall we get Arlene for her birthday?
B: Let's get her some _____ . She likes looking good.
5 A: What shall we get Sayed for his birthday?
B: Let's get him some _____ . He's going to buy a new house.
6 A: What shall we buy for Henrietta?
B: Let's buy her some _____ . She loves silver and gold.

Communication activities

Student A

Factfile

1 Name: Queen Elizabeth
From: the UK
3 Name: Antonio Banderas
From: Spain
5 Name: Jackie Chan
From: China (Hong Kong)

CARD 22

You took a long, expensive holiday. Now you've only got £2,000.
On holiday, you decided to continue your business. You love designing websites! But now you need more money.
What do you want to do?
- I want to borrow money from the bank. (Go to 15 on page 114)
- I don't want to borrow any money. (Go to 18 on page 115)

CARD 23

You decided to think for a while. You talked to your family and friends. They helped you. Now you need to make a decision! What do you want to do?
- I want to invest £8,000 in shares. (Go to 2 on page 96)
- I don't like investing. I want to start a business. (Go to 6 on page 111)

CARD 24

You decided to sell the business, but no one wants to buy it! What do you want to do?
- Close the business. (Go to 7 on page 111)
- Do some market research and find a new direction for your business. (Go to 3 on page 96)

CARD 25

Oh no! That was a mistake! You talked to your uncle, but his business is very slow, too. He can't help you. You lost all your money. The game is over for you.

CARD 26

You designed the website for the company. It was a lot of work. You worked for sixteen hours every day for six months. Now the website is finished. The company is very happy but you've got no friends and a lot of paperwork to do.
What do you want to do?
- Go on holiday. You need it! (Go to 12 on page 113)
- Do the paperwork. (Go to 20 on page 115)

Unit 6 Lesson 3 Exercise 11a

Technology Quiz

1 Have you got a laptop?
YES go to Q3   NO go to Q2

2 Do you want to buy a new laptop?
YES go to Q4   NO go to Q4

3 Is it a new laptop?
YES go to Q4   NO go to Q2

4 Have you got wireless Internet?
YES go to Q6   NO go to Q5

5 Do you want to get wireless Internet at home?
YES go to Q7   NO go to Q7

6 Do you like surfing the Internet on your sofa?
YES go to Q7   NO go to Q7

7 Do you sometimes surf the Internet in bed?
YES go to Q8   NO go to Q8

8 Have you got a big, flat-screen TV?
YES go to Q10   NO go to Q9

9 Do you want to buy a big, flat-screen TV?
YES go to Q10   NO go to Q10

10 Do you sometimes watch TV on your computer?
YES go to Q11   NO go to Q11

11 Have you got a games console?
YES go to Q13   NO go to Q12

12 Do you want to have a games console?
YES go to Q13   NO go to Q14

13 Do you like playing computer games?
YES go to Q14   NO go to Q14

14 Have you got a digital camcorder?
YES go to Q15   NO go to Q16

15 Do you like taking video?
YES go to Q16   NO go to Q16

16 Have you got a mobile phone with a camera?
YES go to Q17   NO go to Q18

17 Do you take a lot of photos with your phone?
YES go to Q18   NO go to Q18

18 Do you like texting?
YES go to Q19   NO go to Q20

19 Do you send more than ten texts a day?
YES go to Q20   NO go to Q20

20 Do you often make video calls on a computer?
YES finished!   NO finished!

Key

What is your score?
Yes = 1 point. No = 0 points.

0-5 points: You don't like new technology. Your photos are in a box – they aren't on a computer. Your music is on CDs. It isn't on an iPod. You don't text and you haven't got wireless Internet.

6-12 points: You like new technology, but you don't love it. You've got a digital camera and you surf the Internet, but you don't surf in bed. You sometimes text your friends.

13+ points: You love technology. All your music and your photos are on your computer. You don't call your friends, you text them. You surf the Internet every day and your mobile phone is very modern.

Unit 9 Communication Exercise 2b

CARD 6

You started your own business. You design websites. You bought a new computer and you rented an office. But business is very slow. You haven't got any customers. Now you only have £5,000.
What do you want to do?
- I want to continue with my business. (Go to 5 on page 96)
- I want to take a long holiday. You only live once! (Go to 22 on page 109)

CARD 7

You closed your business. You aren't an Internet millionaire, but you have free time and friends. The game is over for you.

CARD 8

You gave Sven a job and 30% of your business. That was a good decision. Sven is a good website designer. Now Sven wants to do market research. It costs £10,000!
What do you want to do?
- I want to do market research. It's important. (Go to 3 on page 96)
- I don't want to do market research. It's expensive. (Go to 19 on page 115)

CARD 9

Oh no! That was a mistake! You hired your brother but he isn't very good at business. You haven't got any new customers.
What do you want to do?
- I want to fire my brother and hire Camilla Petrov. (Go to 16 on page 114)
- I don't want to fire my brother. I want to give him another chance. (Go to 14 on page 113)

Unit 10 Lesson 2 Exercise 9a

Complete the questionnaire. Tick (✓) A, B or C.

A = I already do that.
B = I'm going to do that. It's a good idea.
C = I'm not going to do that. It's a silly idea.

Twelve ways to be happy

		A	B	C
1	do regular exercise			
2	sing in the shower			
3	smile a lot			
4	wear yellow clothes			
5	think about now, not the past or the future			
6	buy a new pair of shoes			
7	go for a walk in the countryside			
8	watch a lot of funny films			
9	spend a lot of time with my family			
10	have a plan for the future			
11	look in the mirror and say 'I'm happy to be me'			
12	go to bed early sometimes			

Key

Mostly As: You're a very happy person. You want to be happy – it's very important to you. You don't like being unhappy.

Mostly Bs: Sometimes you're happy and sometimes you're unhappy. That's very normal and you don't mind.

Mostly Cs: You don't like trying to be happy. You think it's silly. You don't like people telling you what to do.

Communication activities

Unit 1 Lesson 2 Exercise 10b
Student B

Factfile
2 Name: Michelle Obama
From: the USA
4 Name: Shakira
From: Colombia
6 Name: Vladimir Putin
From: Russia

Unit 2 Lesson 3 Exercise 9
Student A

Who's she?

Unit 3 Lesson 3 Exercise 10a

Student B

€14.40

€4.99 a bunch

€2.99 a bunch

€35.99

€15.99

€45

€2 each or six for €10

€3.99 a bunch

Unit 9 Communication Exercise 2b

CARD 10

You invested your money. You bought shares in a small company. The shares weren't successful. Now you've got £8,000. What do you want to do?

- I want to invest £8,000 in shares. (Go to 2 on page 96)
- I don't like investing. I want to start a business. (Go to 6 on page 111)
- I don't know what to do. I want to think for a while. (Go to 23 on page 109)

CARD 11

You said yes to the supermarket. That was a mistake. You worked eighteen hours every day for two months, but you didn't finish the work. The supermarket wasn't happy. Your friends weren't happy. You became ill and you stopped working. The game is over for you.

CARD 12

Oh no! That was a mistake! You went on holiday and you didn't do your paperwork. You didn't pay your tax and the taxman closed your business. The game is over for you.

CARD 13

You didn't give Sven a job. That was a mistake because Sven was a good website designer. He isn't happy.
Now a big travel company wants a new website. It's A LOT of work.
What do you want to do?

- I want to call Sven, say sorry and offer him 30% of the company. (Go to 8 on page 111)
- I don't want to call Sven. I want to design the website alone. (Go to 26 on page 109)

CARD 14

Oh no! Another mistake. Your brother is a good artist, but he's a terrible business person. You didn't find any new customers. You lost all your money. The game is over for you.

Unit 10 Lesson 3 Exercise 2a

Student B

Giving presents around the world

When to open the present

Chinese people usually say no three times when you give a gift. Then they say yes, but they open the gift in private. In South America people usually open the present immediately. In Morocco people open the gift later. In Hong Kong, people give the gift with two hands.

What to give

In South Korea a person's first birthday and sixtieth birthday are very important. Korean people often give money on these days. In Cambodia birthdays are not very important. In the UK British people sometimes give just a card and no present. In Saudi Arabia gifts are very important. Saudis only give gifts to very close friends. Gold jewellery isn't a good present for men, but silver is fine. In Colombia people often give gold on a girl's fifteenth birthday.

Unit 9 Lesson 2 Exercise 11a

Student B

In 2005 Anya Peters' temporary job ended. She needed another job, but there weren't any. Anya didn't have any money. She started living in her car. She showered and washed her clothes in public places like hospitals. Anya was homeless, but other people didn't realise.

Anya didn't like her life. She didn't like sleeping in a car. She was often cold and afraid. One day she walked into a public library. There was a computer with free Internet access. Anya started writing a blog. Thousands of people started to read the blog and liked it. Now Anya is a writer. Her book, *Abandoned* was very popular and she has her own house again. 'This is a fantastic second chance,' she says.

Unit 1 Communication Exercise 5

Student B

Name	Sofia
From (country)	the USA
From (city)	New York
Mobile phone number	646 390 150
Home number	212 809 226

Unit 9 Communication Exercise 2b

CARD 15

You borrowed £50,000 from the bank. That was a good decision!
Two weeks ago, you met another website designer, Sven. He is very good. You want to give Sven a job, but Sven wants 30% of your business. What do you want to do?
- I want to give Sven a job and give him 30% of my business. (Go to 8 on page 111)
- I don't want to give Sven a job. (Go to 13 on page 113)

CARD 16

You hired a new sales manager. Her name is Camilla Petrov. That was a good decision. Now you have a lot of work. Last month you earned a lot of money but you worked sixteen hours a day. You didn't see your friends and you weren't happy. Now a big electronics company wants a new website. It's A LOT of work.
What do you want to do?
- I don't like working really hard. I want to sell the business. (Go to 24 on page 109)
- I want to design the website for the electronics company. (Go to 26 on page 109)

CARD 17

You made the right decision. You went to night school and you learned to write apps. You wrote some very popular apps. Last year your business earned £1,500,000. You are now an Internet millionaire! Congratulations!

Unit 2 Lesson 2 Exercise 9

Unit 9 Communication Exercise 2b

CARD 18

You didn't borrow any money from the bank. That was a mistake! Every business needs money. Now you need a sales manager. Two people want the job, your brother (he's an artist, not a business person) and Camilla Petrov (she's a good business person, but she isn't family).
What do you want to do?
- I want to hire my brother. (Go to 9 on page 111)
- I want to hire Camilla Petrov. (Go to 16 on page 114)

CARD 19

You didn't do market research. That was a mistake. Sven was unhappy and he quit. Your business is very slow.
What do you want to do?
- I want to change my mind. I want to do market research. (Go to 3 on page 96)
- I want to hire a sales manager (Go to 16 on page 114)

CARD 20

You didn't go on holiday. You stayed at home and you did the paperwork for your business. It wasn't fun, but it was important.
Now you are very tired, but a big supermarket wants a new website! This is A LOT of work and a lot of money. What do you want to do?
- Say yes to the supermarket. (Go to 11 on page 113)
- Say no to the supermarket. (Go to 4 on page 96)

CARD 21

You didn't go to night school. Business is very slow. Now you have £5,000 in the bank. What do you want to do?
- I change my mind! I want to go to night school and learn to write apps. (Go to 17 on page 114)
- I want to talk to my rich uncle. Maybe he can help. (Go to 25 on page 109)

Communication activities

Unit 1 Lesson 3 Exercise 10a

Survey

Name	My answers		
What's your favourite ...			
film?			
football team?			
food?			
book?			
Who's your favourite ...			
fashion designer?			
singer?			
actor?			

Unit 1 Communication Exercise 5

Student C

Name	Marta
From (country)	Spain
From (city)	Madrid
Mobile phone number	691 439 0023
Home number	914 710 430

Unit 2 Lesson 1 Exercise 10

Student B

Zara Phillips, cousin of William and Harry

Prince Edward and Sophie, uncle and aunt of William and Harry

Prince William and Prince Harry

Queen Elizabeth, grandmother of William and Harry

Prince Charles, father of William and Harry

Princess Beatrice and Princess Eugenie, cousins of William and Harry

Unit 4 Lesson 3 Exercise 7b
Student B

Shinjuku Station

There are over 300 train stations in Tokyo. Shinjuku station is the biggest. There are over 3,000,000 (three million) passengers every day. There are also hundreds of shops in the station. It's open 24 hours a day but the morning rush hour is from 7 o'clock to 9:30 and the evening rush hour is from 3:30 to 10 o'clock. Shinjuku station is about 125 years old.

1   Where is the station?
2   When is it open?
3   When is the morning rush hour?
4   When is the evening rush hour?
5   Are there a lot of passengers?
6   Is it old?

Unit 2 Lesson 3 Exercise 9
Student B

Who's he?

Communication activities

Unit 1 Communication Exercise 5

Student A

Name	Leonardo
From (country)	Mexico
From (city)	Mexico City
Mobile phone number	556 893 2085
Home number	556 933 2107

Unit 7 Lesson 1 Exercise 11

	Love	Like	Quite like	Don't mind	Don't like	Hate
play	football			golf		
do						
go						
singers/actors						
places						
bands						

Unit 9 Lesson 2 Exercise 11a

Student A

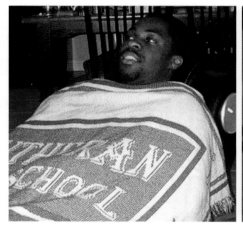

In 2004 Vaughan Bailey's parents divorced. Vaughan was sixteen. He didn't want to live with his mother or father, so he lived on the streets. He didn't work or study, he just played basketball. Vaughan was broke. 'Life was very, very difficult.' Then Vaughan's life started to change. He played basketball for a local team. Then he played for England.

In 2009 Vaughan injured his leg. He was very upset but he didn't panic. He changed his job. Vaughan started working as a model. In 2010 he entered the *Mr England* competition. Vaughan was the winner! Now he is a celebrity, a successful model, an actor and a TV presenter. 'It's like a dream,' he says.

Unit 10 Lesson 3 Exercise 2a

Student A

Giving presents around the world

The number of presents

In Japan presents are very important and Japanese people like giving them. They don't give four things (e.g. four glasses) as a gift – it's unlucky. Nine is also unlucky. In Italy and Poland people usually give odd numbers of flowers (1, 3, 5, etc). In China they always give even numbers of flowers (2, 4, 6, etc). In South Korea people sometimes give seven things because it's lucky.

Important colours

In Germany flowers are a good gift, but not red roses. They are for lovers. In Vietnam black is an unlucky colour, so don't give presents in black wrapping paper. In China red wrapping paper is good, but yellow is bad. In India yellow, green and red are lucky colours, so choose those for wrapping paper.

Unit 8 Lesson 3 Exercise 9a

1   The River Thames is 346 kilometres long.
2   The Eiffel Tower is 324 metres tall.
3   It is 3,200 kilometres from Perth to the nearest big city (Adelaide).
4   The flight from New York to Madrid is seven hours.
5   The Mediterranean is 1,500 metres deep, on average.
6   A sixty kilogram person is ten kilograms on the moon.

Can do complete simple sentences about your favourite things

Nine Facts About Me

Apple is my favourite type of mobile phone,
Pizza is my favourite **food** when I'm at home.
Madrid is my favourite capital **city**,
Japan is my favourite foreign country.
Twenty is my favourite age (so far),
Mercedes is my favourite type of **car**.
Twitter.com is my favourite **website**,
Casablanca is my favourite film in black and white.
Football is my favourite sport on TV.
And that's the end of Nine Facts About Me.

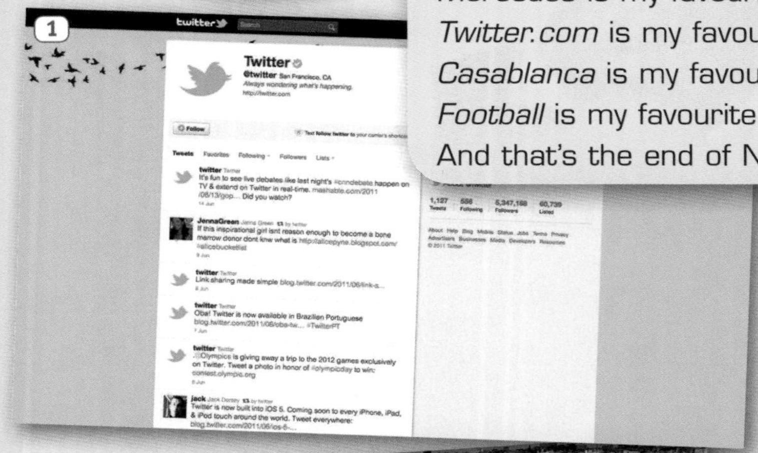

1 Read the poem. Match the words in **bold** with the photos.

1 = website

2 **a** Read the poem again. Tick (✓) the lines that are true for you.

b Work in pairs. Ask questions about the things in the poem.

A: *Is Apple your favourite type of mobile phone?*

B: *No, it isn't. Nokia is my favourite type of mobile phone.*

3 **a** Read the How to... box.

How to... spell consonant sounds in English

sound /k/ → spelling = *c, k* or *ck*.
car bank black

sound /s/ → spelling = *s, ss* or *c*.
sport passport city

sound /dʒ/ → spelling = *j, g* or *ge*.
Japan Germany age

sound /f/ → spelling = *f, ff* or *ph*.
football off phone

b How do you say the letters in red?

1 doctor
2 cinema
3 clock
4 France
5 restaurant
6 John
7 George
8 film
9 photo

4 Look at the poem again. Change the words in *italics*. Make the poem true for you.

Blackberry is my favourite type of mobile phone,
Chocolate is my favourite food when I'm at home.

5 Work in pairs. Read your poems out loud.

2 An email

Can do write short, simple phrases about a family photo

From: jamiewest@westmail.net
To: franz@ihpindustries.de
Subject: Hi!
Attachments: myfamily.jpg

Hi Franz,

How are you? Long time, no see! I'm a teacher at the Technical University in Berlin now. It's a great city but I'm only here for six months! Where are you now?

The attachment is a photo of my family. I'm with Ingrid, my wife. The children are Karina, Dirk and Freya. Karina's five, Dirk's seven and Freya's two. The old couple are my parents, Bill and Sue. It's hot in the photo but it's cold in Berlin!

Hope to hear from you soon.

Jamie

1 Read the email and label the people in the photo.

2 a Read the How to... box.

> ### How to... use *and* and *but*
>
> We use *and*
> - before the last item in a list
> *The children are Karina, Dirk **and** Freya.*
> - to join similar sentences
> *Karina's five. Dirk's seven. Freya's two.* →
> *Karina's five, Dirk's seven **and** Freya's two.*
>
> We use *but*
> - to join different sentences
> *It's a great city **but** I'm only here for six months!*

b <u>Underline</u> more examples of *and* and *but* in the email.

3 Rewrite the sentences with *and* or *but* in the correct place.

1 My sisters are Jessica, Julie, Jane.
My sisters are Jessica, Julie and Jane.
2 Hans is my brother. Konrad isn't my brother.
3 My mother is sixty-one. My father is sixty-two.
4 My children are five, seven, ten.
5 I'm in London. My family is in New York.

4 Imagine the people in this photo are your family. Complete the information about each person.

	Name	Relationship to you	Age
1			
2			
3			

5 Write an email to a friend and describe the photo.

To: Natasha
Cc:
Subject: My family

Hi Natasha,
How are you? Long time, no see!
The attachment is a photo of my family. The old man is ... . The young man is ... and the boy is ... .
It's ... in the photo but ...
Hope to hear from you soon,

Della's Bargain Shop
The web's best bargains!

Basket

Sign in

Help

Kitchen
- Glasses
- Knives
- more

Jewellery
- Watches
- Rings
- more

Books
- Dictionaries
- Novels
- more

Bargain of the week

Bargain of the week 1
Bel-Vere glasses
€19.99
NOW €9.99
Read reviews
Buy now!

Bargain of the week 2
S-presso coffee machine
€129.99
NOW €64.99
Read reviews
Buy now!

Bargain of the week 3
Kitchen Kendo Knives
€89.99
NOW €79.99
Read reviews
Buy now!

1 What do you buy online? Make a list.

CDs, DVDs ...

2 Look at the website. Are the items bargains?

The glasses are a bargain. They're beautiful and they're cheap.

3 Complete the reviews with the correct word: *glasses, coffee machine* or *knives*.

★★★★☆ This is an OK (1) _____ . It's small and it's fast and it's half price now. So what's the problem? It's not very beautiful.

★★★★★ These coloured (2) _____ are great. They're expensive and they're quite small, but they're very nice. Five stars!

★★☆☆☆ These (3) _____ are expensive, but they aren't very good. Try Le Chop. Their (4) _____ are really good and they're only €50!

★★★★★ This is a great (5) _____ . It's expensive, but it's very fast and very good. Five stars!

★★★★☆ These (6) _____ are very nice and now they're only €10! What a bargain!

★★★★★ These black (7) _____ are great. They're expensive, but they're easy to use.

4 Read the How to... box. Complete the examples with words from the website.

> ### How to... spell noun plurals
>
> 1 Most nouns
>   add **-s** plates, saucepans
>
> 2 Nouns that end in *-ch, -sh, -s* or *-x*
>   add **-es** watches, (a) _____
>
> 3 Nouns that end in *-f* or *-fe*
>   replace *-f* or *-fe* with **-ves**
>   wife → wives,
>   (b) _____ → _____
>
> 4 Nouns that end in consonant + *y*
>   change consonant + *-y* to **-ies**
>   party → parties, (c) _____ → _____

5 Correct the sentences.

1 Elena and Kim are babys.

2 Rodrigo and Juan are good boyes.

3 Those are my brushs.

4 These are English dictionarys.

5 Are these your keyes?

6 Write online reviews for three things in your house. Give each thing 1–5 stars.

★★☆☆☆ *This Deltran computer isn't very good. It's expensive and it's very slow.*

4 An online profile update

Can do write a simple online profile update

FriendsConnect

Search

Hasina Kareem Profile Friends Photos +

What's on your mind?   Share

City
New York

Married
No

Birthday
5th April

Hasina Kareem It's day three of our holiday and we're in Damascus. It's my parents' favourite city. They're really happy here. It's a beautiful city – the 'City of Jasmine'. There are fantastic palaces and markets here and our hotel is close to the Barada River. It's very hot (and it's only half past nine in the morning!), but there's air conditioning in our hotel ☺. There are about two million people in Damascus and my dad is friends with most of them already!

July 12th at 9:35 a.m.

Damascus

1 Do you have an online profile? Do your friends have profiles?

2 a Read Hasina's profile. Where is she?

b Read the profile again and answer the questions.
1 Who is Hasina with?
2 What is another name for Damascus?
3 Where is Hasina's hotel?
4 What time is it?
5 How many people are there in Damascus?

3 a Read the How to... box.

How to... use capital letters and full stops

We use a capital letter at the start of a sentence. We use a full stop at the end of a sentence.
We also use capital letters for ...
• names: *Hasina*
• countries, cities, rivers, mountains: *Damascus*, *Syria*
• languages and nationalities: *Syrian*, *English*

b Add full stops and capital letters to Hasina's next update.

Hasina Kareem it's day ten of our holiday and we're in amman in jordan amman is a city on nineteen hills it's different to damascus but it's really beautiful too the language here is arabic there are a lot of writers and artists here there are a lot of museums too

July 19th at 10:15 a.m.

4 Imagine you are a tourist in your town. It's the first day of your holiday. Complete the details.
City
beautiful ☐   OK ☐   ugly ☐
Attractions
(L = a lot of; S = some; O = one; N = none)
palaces ☐   rivers ☐   museums ☐
markets ☐   shops ☐   parks ☐
Weather
hot ☐   warm ☐   cool ☐   cold ☐

5 a Now write a profile update for your friends.

It's day one of my holiday and I'm in ... . It's a ... city. There are a lot of ... and there's a great ... . Our hotel is close to ... . It's very ... here at the moment.

b Read your update. Check for capital letters and full stops. Then give your update to another student. Read their update. Is it similar to yours?

123

me ↓

1 Work in pairs and answer the questions.

Do you have a pen friend?

Yes → Tell your partner about your pen friend.

No → Do you want a pen friend?

2 Read the letter. Who are the people in the photo? Who is Lemal?

3 Read the letter again and answer the questions.

1 Where is Lemal from?

2 Where does Beth go to school?

3 What does she do at the weekend?

4 a Read the How to... box.

How to... use common letter phrases

Start a letter

Dear [Lemal/Grandpa/Mrs Smith]

Thank you for [your letter].

End a letter

I hope to hear from you soon.

Best wishes, [your name]

---

b Add phrases to Lemal's letter.

(1) _____ ,

(2) _____ . I love your photo. Your sisters are really beautiful.

My brother, Dominick, is very tall and thin, too.

(3) _____ .

(4) _____ ,

Lemal

5 Complete the sentences about you.

1 I live with ... . He/She/They is/are ...

2 I work for .../I study ...

3 In the morning I ...

4 In the evening I ...

5 At the weekend I ...

6 Now write a letter to a new pen friend. Write about you and your family.

18th October

Dear Lemal,

Thank you for your letter and photograph. I'm really happy to have a new pen friend from South Africa! Here's some information about me and my family.

My full name's Beth Westwood and I live in a small house in Edinburgh, Scotland. I live with my mum and dad, and my sisters, Abby and Liz. Dad's got fair hair and he's a bit fat, but Mum and my sisters are tall and thin.

I go to school in Edinburgh. I get up at 7:30 in the morning! In the afternoon I come home and do my homework. In the evening I surf the Internet or read a book. On Saturdays we all go out for dinner. I love pasta, but Mum and Dad like fish and chips. On Sundays I get up very late.

I hope to hear from you soon.

Best wishes,

Beth

Can do | complete simple sentences about someone's typical day

A day in the life of my neighbour, Maurice

My friend Maurice has a very _____ life. He works from home. He gets up late every morning. He has a shower **and then** he has breakfast. **After that** he has a coffee and he reads a newspaper. **Then** he starts work. In the afternoon he often sleeps for one or two hours. He doesn't usually do housework and he never cooks. He finishes work around six o'clock **and then**, in the evening, he watches TV or he goes out with his friends. Sometimes I want Maurice's life!

1 **a** Think about your friends and family. Who has a very easy life? Who has a hard life?

  b Work in pairs. Tell your partner your answers to exercise 1a.

2 **a** Read the text. Complete the first sentence with *easy* or *difficult*.

  b Read the text again. Are the sentences true (T), false (F) or not given (NG)?

  1 Maurice gets up around nine o'clock. ☐
  2 He likes coffee. ☐
  3 He hasn't got a job. ☐
  4 He is married. ☐
  5 He eats out in the evenings. ☐

3 Read the How to... box.

> ## How to... use *then* and *after that*
>
> Use *then* and *after that* to put events in order.
> *He has a shower **and then** he has breakfast.*
> *... he has breakfast. **After that** he has a coffee.*
> *... and he reads a newspaper. **Then** he starts work.*

4 Complete the sentences with *then*, *and then* or *after that*.

  1 I get up at seven o'clock. _____ I have a shower.
  2 My husband finishes work around seven _____ _____ he comes home.
  3 We usually watch a film _____ _____ we go to bed.
  4 She has lunch at one o'clock. _____ she starts work again.

5 **a** Choose a person from exercise 1a. Complete the sentences about him/her.

  1 He/She gets up around ... . Then he/she ... .
  2 In the afternoon he/she ... . After that, he/she ... .
  3 In the evening he/she ... and then he/she ... .

  b Write a short text about a typical day in his/her life. Use the sentences in exercise 5a. Add some details.

  My friend Daniella has a very difficult life. She ...

Can do | use common phrases to complete a simple email invitation

1 Work in pairs. How do you make arrangements with your friends?

> by email   by telephone   by text
> face to face   online

I make arrangements face to face.

2 **a** Read the email. What does Rebecca want to celebrate?

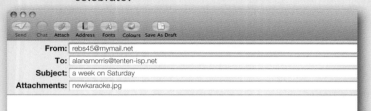

From: rebs45@mymail.net
To: alanamorris@tenten-isp.net
Subject: a week on Saturday
Attachments: newkaraoke.jpg

Hi Alana,

How are you? I hope you're well. How are things at work? Everything's fine here. I have my last Law exam next week, so I'm really busy at the moment.

Are you free on Saturday 14th? I want to celebrate the end of my exams. Why don't we hire a car and go to the beach for the day? I can't drive, but you can. There's a new karaoke bar near the beach (see the attachment). Let's go there in the evening. I know, I know, I can't sing, but ... it's fun to try!

Let me know.

Love,

Rebecca

b Read the email again. Then complete the sentences with a name, Rebecca or Alana.

1 _____ is a Law student.
2 _____ has got a job.
3 _____ can drive.
4 _____ can't sing.

3 **a** Read the How to... box.

How to... use common email phrases

To start an email	*How are things?*
	I hope you're well.
To invite a friend to do something	*Are you free next/on Saturday?*
	Why don't we [hire a car]?
	Let's go [to the beach].
End an email	*Let me know.*
	Love,
	All the best,

b Which phrases from the box can you find in Rebecca's email?

4 Complete the email with phrases from the How to... box.

To: Jun-Yi
Cc:
Subject: How are you?

Hi Jun-Yi,

How (1) _____ _____ ? I (2) _____ _____ _____ . I'm fine, but I'm quite tired.

Are (3) _____ _____ _____ Friday evening? It's my birthday. (4) _____ _____ _____ go out for a meal? (5) _____ go to that new Chinese restaurant on Laurel Street.

(6) _____ _____ _____

(7) _____ ,

Chelsea

5 **a** It's your birthday next Saturday. How do you want to celebrate?

b Write an email to your best friend. Invite him or her to do something on your birthday. Use the email in exercise 4 to help you.

A Short Biography of ...

Billie Holiday

Billie Holiday was a great jazz singer and songwriter. She was born on 7th April 1915 in Philadelphia. When she was a child, she was angry and unhappy. Her father was never at home and her family was poor. She was also unhappy when she was famous. She was a drug addict and her marriages weren't successful. But Billie Holiday's music was incredible and her songs *Strange Fruit* and *Lady Sings the Blues* are jazz classics. Holiday was just 44 when she died.

1 **a** Work in pairs. What do you know about the woman in the photo?

b Read the short biography of Billie Holiday. When did she die?

2 Read the biography again. Are the statements true (T) or false (F)?

1 Billie Holiday was born in the USA. ☐
2 When she was a child, she was rich. ☐
3 Her father was a good dad. ☐
4 She wasn't married. ☐
5 *Strange Fruit* is one of her famous songs. ☐

3 Read the How to... box.

> ### How to... join clauses with *when*
>
> *When* he was a child, he was happy.
> *When* they were teenagers, they were at my school.
> I was good at sport *when* I was at school.
> She was poor *when* she was a child.

4 Join the clauses in two ways with *when*.

1 I was a child/I was happy
When I was a child, I was happy.
I was happy when I was a child.
2 she was young/she was always late
3 you were a teenager/you were a great singer
4 we were best friends/we were teenagers

5 **a** Use the table to write sentences about you with *when*.

When I was a child, When I was a teenager, When I was at school,	I was always/never in trouble. I was good/bad at (English). I was/wasn't very happy. my best friend was ... my life was really good/bad.

b Work in pairs and compare your sentences.

6 **a** Work in pairs. Think of a famous person who is dead. Complete the sentences about him/her.

1 He/She was born in ...
2 When he/she was a child, ...
3 When he/she was famous, ...
4 He/She was ... years old when he/she died.

b Now write a short biography about your famous person. Use the sentences in exercise 6a and add some more information.

1 **a** What blogs do you read? Do you read them in English?

  b Look at Matt's blog. Who do you think reads it?

2 Read Matt's blog. Answer the questions.

  1 What did Lester lend Matt?
  2 What happened to them?
  3 Where did Matt find them?
  4 Where did Matt go on Tuesday?

Matt's Week
A good week and a bad week

Posted by Matt at 08:01 a.m. on Friday

I had a terrible day on Monday. I borrowed some DVDs from my friend, Lester. I borrowed *The Wire*, *Mad Men* and *House*. When I got home, the DVDs weren't in my bag! Lester wasn't very happy.

I had a great day on Tuesday. I found Lester's DVDs. They were in my coat pocket. In the evening I went out with my friend, Claire. We had dinner in a restaurant.

3 Read the How to... box.

How to... use commas (,) and apostrophes (')

We use commas
- in lists
I borrowed The Wire, Mad Men *and* House.
- to give extra information, e.g. names
I borrowed some DVDs from my friend, Lester.

We use apostrophes
- for contractions
The DVDs weren't in my bag.
- with *s* to show possession
I found Lester's DVDs.

---

4 Add commas and apostrophes to this blog.

Marys blog

Posted by Mary at 12:10 a.m. on Monday

I had a great day on Saturday. It was Bens birthday. Ben Sally and I had dinner at Emmas house. We ate pizza pasta and garlic bread. Delicious!

I had a terrible day on Sunday. I borrowed a jacket from my sister Yasmin but I lost it. I think I left it at the café near Bens flat. Yasmin wasn't happy.

5 **a** Think about last week. Write one good event and one bad event.
Good: I had a great meal in a restaurant.
Bad: ...

  b Write a blog about last week. Tell your friends about the good event and the bad event.
I had a terrible day on Wednesday. I ...

Can do | write a text to a friend using common text expressions

1 Work in pairs and answer the questions.
1 How many text messages do you send every day?
2 What common text expressions are there in your language?

2 **a** Read six text messages (A–F). Put them in order.

b Answer the questions.
1 What is Lance going to do tomorrow night?
2 What are Lance and Nina going to do next week?
3 Where are they going to meet, and when?

3 **a** Read the How to... box.

> **How to... use SMS (texting) language**
>
> We only use SMS/text language with friends.
> You can leave out some words,
> e.g. *there is/are.*
> *no tickets left! = There are no tickets left!*
> You can use single letters, numbers or symbols, e.g.
>
> b = *be*   c = *see*   u = *you*   @ = *at*
> 2 = *to*   4 = *for*   RU = *Are you*   Gr8 = *great*

b Rewrite the text messages in exercise 2a as full sentences.

E   Hi Lance. Are you free tomorrow? I want to see the new Monet exhibition at the National Gallery.

4 Make these sentences into text messages.
1 How are you? I'm great!
2 See you later!
3 Do you want to meet for dinner?
4 What are you going to do?
5 I'll see you at the cinema at eight o'clock. Don't be late!

5 Work in pairs. Write texts to each other.
Student A: invite Student B to have dinner with you. You are only free on Friday nights.
Student B: Reply to Student A's text. Try to find a time to have dinner with him/her. You are not free this week but you are free next week.

A Sat fine. CU @ gallery @ 1pm?

B Hi Nina. Sorry, can't. Going to have dinner with Henry.

C Gr8! CU then.

D OK. Never mind. Next week?

E Hi Lance. RU free 2mrow? I want 2 c new Monet exhibition @ National Gallery.

F Next Sat is good 4 me. U?

Pronunciation bank

Phonetic chart

Vowels	ɪ	e	ʊ	uː	æ	ɑː
	it	pen	put	do	bag	hard
	iː	ə	ɜː	ɔː	ʌ	ɒ
	she	under	her	four	does	shop

Diphthongs	ɪə	eə	eɪ	ɔɪ	aɪ	aʊ	əʊ
	here	there	play	boy	my	now	no

Consonants	p	t	k	tʃ	f	θ	s	ʃ
	pizza	taxi	coffee	chocolate	film	three	salad	shoe
	b	d	g	dʒ	v	ð	z	ʒ
	bus	doctor	girl	Germany	van	that	zoo	television
	m	n	ŋ	h	l	r	j	w
	man	nice	sing	hot	like	red	young	wife

Minimal pairs 🔊 2.64

	Phonetic symbol	Example	Phonetic symbol	Example	Sentence
1	/ɪ/	big	/æ/	bag	It's a big bag.
2	/ɪ/	sit	/iː/	seat	Can I sit in this seat?
3	/æ/	map	/ɒ/	mop	That's my map and my mop.
4	/ɪ/	live	/ʌ/	love	I love living in London.
5	/ʌ/	cup	/æ/	cap	The cup is under your cap.
6	/iː/	me	/ɔː/	more	Please give me more.
7	/ɪ/	ship	/ɒ/	shop	There's a shop on the ship.
8	/ɪ/	lift	/e/	left	The lift is on the left.
9	/ɑː/	car	/iː/	key	Where's my car key?
10	/ɒ/	box	/ʊ/	books	Look at the box of books.
11	/iː/	he	/ɜː/	her	He hates her.
12	/iː/	Sophie	/ə/	sofa	Sophie's on the sofa.
13	/e/	let	/eɪ/	late	Let's get up late.
14	/aɪ/	kite	/eɪ/	Kate	This is Kate's kite.
15	/iː/	she	/əʊ/	show	She's at the show.
16	/iː/	eat	/eɪ/	eight	Did Jane eat eight cakes?
17	/aʊ/	how	/aɪ/	Hi	Hi. How are you?
18	/iː/	week	/eɪ/	wake	I wake up at six in the week.
19	/p/	Paul	/b/	ball	Put Paul's ball in the bin.
20	/t/	to	/d/	do	What do you want to do?
21	/k/	came	/g/	game	He came and played a game.
22	/tʃ/	chess	/dʒ/	Jess	Jess plays chess.
23	/f/	off	/v/	of	Please get off of Fran's van.
24	/p/	pink	/θ/	think	I think it's pink.
25	/p/	pay	/ð/	they	Did they pay for the party?
26	/s/	keeps	/z/	keys	She keeps her keys in her bag.
27	/t/	fit	/ʃ/	fish	Is your fish fit?
28	/t/	letter	/ʒ/	leisure	This letter's about leisure.
29	/m/	mice	/n/	nice	Are your mice nice?
30	/l/	collect	/r/	correct	Did you collect the correct letter?

Pronunciation bank

Sound-spelling correspondences

Sound	Spelling	Examples
/ɪ/	i	this listen
	y	gym typical
	ui	build guitar
	e	pretty
/iː/	ee	green sleep
	ie	niece believe
	ea	read teacher
	e	these complete
	ey	key money
	ei	receipt receive
	i	police
/æ/	a	can man pasta land
/ɑː/	a	can't dance*
	ar	scarf bargain
	al	half
	au	aunt laugh
	ea	heart
/ʌ/	u	fun sunny husband
	o	some mother month
	ou	cousin double young
/ɒ/	o	hot pocket top
	a	watch what want

Sound	Spelling	Examples
/ɔː/	or	short sport store
	ou	your course bought
	au	daughter taught
	al	bald small always
	aw	draw jigsaw
	ar	warm
	oo	floor indoor
/aɪ/	i	like time island
	y	dry shy cycle
	ie	fries die tie
	igh	light high right
	ei	height
	ey	eyes
	uy	buy
/eɪ/	a	lake hate
	ai	wait train straight
	ay	play say stay
	ey	they grey obey
	ei	eight weight
	ea	break
/əʊ/	o	home phone open
	ow	show throw own
	oa	coat road coast
	ol	cold told

* In American English the sound in words like *can't* and *dance* is the /æ/ sound, like *can* and *man*.

Syllable stress ● 2.65

one-syllable words
●

one six big young read
learn friend great lake
house beach road west

two-syllable words
●○

happy seven listen
morning passport father
website surname photo
awful teacher picture
modern Sunday

two-syllable words
○●

Japan address between today
return behind Chinese
design July explain
mistake dessert because

three-syllable words
●○○

India favourite gallery holiday
beautiful Saturday visitor
newsagent medium popular
opposite interview architect
hospital

three-syllable words
○●○

eleven computer cathedral
espresso attachment
important piano designer
reporter together September
tomorrow exciting potato

three-syllable words
○○●

afternoon engineer introduce
magazine

Irregular verbs

Verb	Past Simple	Past Participle
be	was/were	been
become	became	become
begin	began	begun
break	broke	broken
bring	brought	brought
build	built	built
buy	bought	bought
can	could	been able
catch	caught	caught
choose	chose	chosen
come	came	come
cost	cost	cost
dig	dug	dug
do	did	done
draw	drew	drawn
drink	drank	drunk
drive	drove	driven
eat	ate	eaten
fall	fell	fallen
feed	fed	fed
feel	felt	felt
find	found	found
fly	flew	flown
forget	forgot	forgotten
get	got	got
give	gave	given
go	went	gone/been
grow	grew	grown
have	had	had
hear	heard	heard
hold	held	held
hurt	hurt	hurt
keep	kept	kept
know	knew	known
learn	learned/learnt	learned/learnt

Verb	Past Simple	Past Participle
leave	left	left
let	let	let
lose	lost	lost
make	made	made
mean	meant	meant
meet	met	met
pay	paid	paid
put	put	put
read/ri:d/	read/red/	read/red/
ride	rode	ridden
ring	rang	rung
run	ran	run
say	said	said
see	saw	seen
sell	sold	sold
send	sent	sent
shine	shone	shone
show	showed	shown
sing	sang	sung
sit	sat	sat
sleep	slept	slept
speak	spoke	spoken
spend	spent	spent
stand	stood	stood
steal	stole	stolen
swim	swam	swum
take	took	taken
teach	taught	taught
tell	told	told
think	thought	thought
throw	threw	thrown
understand	understood	understood
wear	wore	worn
win	won	won
write	wrote	written

Audioscripts

Do you know...?

Track 1.01
1 read
2 write
3 speak
4 listen
5 match
6 repeat
7 look
8 choose
9 complete

Track 1.02
1 Can you repeat that, please?
2 What's *Hola* in English?
3 Sorry, I don't understand.
4 What does *complete* mean?
5 Can you help me, please?
6 What's the answer to number 4?

Unit 1

Track 1.03
bank, bus, café, chocolate, cinema, coffee, computer, doctor, film, football, hotel, Internet, passport, pizza, police, restaurant, salad, student, taxi, telephone, television, university

Track 1.04
1
A: Hi. I'm Kate. What's your name?
B: My name's Clive.
A: Nice to meet you.
B: Nice to meet you, too.
2
A: Hello, Mr Smith. I'm Doctor Mazur.
B: Hello. Nice to meet you.
A: Nice to meet you, too.
3
A: Hello.
B: Hello. My name's Iris Salas.
A: Welcome to Hotel Panorama, Ms Salas.
B: Thank you.
A: You're in room 3–1–5.

Track 1.05
/aɪ/ Hi, I, Clive, Iris, nice, my

Track 1.06
Clive: Hi, I'm Clive.
Iris: Hi Clive. My name's Iris.
Clive: Nice to meet you.
Iris: Nice to meet you, too.

Track 1.07
zero, oh, one, two, three, four, five, six, seven, eight, nine, ten

Track 1.08
1 Nice to meet you.
2 Hello. I'm Paul Smith.
3 Welcome to Hotel Panorama.
4 Hi. What's your name?

Track 1.09
Mike: Look, Nora! It's a quiz.
Nora: Is it a celebrity quiz?

Mike: No, it isn't. It's a fashion quiz. Question one. Who's he? Is he Calvin Klein or Giorgio Armani?
Nora: He's Giorgio Armani.
Mike: Correct! And where's he from? Spain or Italy?
Nora: He's from Italy.
Mike: Very good. Question two. Who's she?
Nora: Er ... is she Donatella Versace?
Mike: No, she isn't. She's Donna Karan. And where is Donna Karan from?
Nora: Well, she isn't from the UK so ... she's from the USA.
Mike: Correct! Question three. Who's he?
Nora: Hm ... is he Jimmy Choo?
Mike: Yes, he is. Where's he from?
Nora: He's from Malaysia.
Mike: That's right. Well done. You're a fashion expert!

Track 1.10
Argentina, Brazil, China, France, Germany, India, Italy, Japan, Mexico, Poland, Russia, Spain, the UK, the USA

Track 1.11
A: Where are you from, Becky?
B: I'm from the USA.
A: Where in the USA?
B: New York.

Track 1.12
I'm, you're, he's, she's, it's, isn't, who's, where's

Track 1.13
1 I'm from Spain and she's from China.
2 It isn't a film quiz. It's a fashion quiz.
3 Who's he? He isn't a student.
4 She's from Germany and she's in room three.
5 Where's she from? Is she from Poland?

Track 1.14
Brazil	Brazilian
Germany	German
India	Indian
Italy	Italian
Mexico	Mexican
Russia	Russian
the USA	American
Poland	Polish
Spain	Spanish
the UK	British
China	Chinese
Japan	Japanese

Track 1.15
1 729 1553
2 07863 400212
3 01873 839711

Track 1.16
1 My mobile number is 0583 121 558.
2 My home number is 422 81009.
3 My work number is 01472 698471.

Track 1.17
1
A: What's your phone number, James?
B: My mobile number is 0747 499109.
A: Sorry, can you say that again?
B: Yes. It's 0747 499109.
A: Great. Thanks.
2
A: What's the number?
B: It's 0208 114 9032.
A: Is it a work number or a home number?
B: I don't know.
3
A: What's your number, Julia?
B: It's 0118 887 3374.
A: Sorry. Could you repeat that?
B: Yes. It's 0118 887 3374.
A: Thanks.

Track 1.18
A: What's your mobile number?
B: It's 0749 128384.
A: Sorry. Can you say that again?
B: Yes, it's 0749 128384. And my work number is 01532 229150.
A: Sorry. Could you repeat that?
B: Yes, it's 01532 229150.
A: Thanks.

Unit 2

Track 1.19
aunt, boyfriend, brother, cousin, daughter, father, friend, girlfriend, grandfather, grandmother, husband, mother, sister, son, uncle, wife

Track 1.20
a, e, i, o, u

Track 1.21
a b c d e f g h i j k l m n o p q r s t u v w x y z

Track 1.22
A: What's your name?
B: Billy.
A: How do you spell that?
B: B–I–double L–Y.

Track 1.23
Dialogue 1
A: Hi Mum. Are we late?
B: No, you aren't. Come in, Hiro.
A: Mum, Dad, this is Alice, my new girlfriend.
B: Nice to meet you, Alice.
C: Nice to meet you, too, Mrs Tanaka.
Dialogue 2
A: Are Grandma and Grandpa here?
B: Yes, they are. They're outside with Baby Boris.
A: Baby Boris? Who's Baby Boris?
B: Not who – what. It's their new sports car.
Dialogue 3
A: This is Alfie. He's Helen's new boyfriend.
B: Hello Alfie. I'm Liz and this is my sister, Mina. Nice to meet you.

C: Nice to meet you, too. Is Helen your friend?

B: No, she isn't. She's our cousin.

Track 1.24

1 We're brother and sister.
2 **A:** Are you married?
   B: Yes, we are.
3 **A:** Are they in the garden?
   B: No, they aren't.
4 We aren't late.
5 They aren't Chinese.
6 We're from Poland.
7 **A:** Are you late?
   B: No, we aren't.
8 We're from Moscow.
9 They're in love.

Track 1.25

1 **Peter:** How do you spell your names?
   Ian: I'm Ian, I–A–N, and she's Ruth, R–U–T–H.
2 **Adam:** I'm Adam and this is my brother, Ben.
   Ben: And this is our mother, Barbara.
3 **Carol:** Lisa and Fran are sisters.
   Bob: Is Alan their father?
   Carol: No, he isn't. He's their uncle.
4 **Andy:** Hi, Olga. Hi, Natalia. Where are your passports?
   Olga: They're in my bag.

Track 1.26

apple, book, brush, business card, camera, computer, iPod, key, mobile, orange, passport, pen, purse, ticket, umbrella, watch

Track 1.27

/æ/ apple, camera, grandpa, café, bag
/e/ pen, Internet, umbrella, friend, seven

Track 1.28

1 My camera and my umbrella are in my bag.
2 I'm in a taxi and my friend is in a café.
3 What's in my bag? Ten pens and an apple.

Track 1.29

Lilly: Hi. I'm Lilly. I'm half Chinese, half British. What's in my bag? Well, a computer and a mobile phone, of course. And two passports – my Chinese passport and my British passport. And my keys, two brushes, my purse, an umbrella and ... and a business card.

Jeff: Hello. I'm Jeff. I'm American. What's in my bag? Er ... an apple, two oranges, an iPod for my music ... and a book – *Catch 22* by Joseph Heller. It's a great book. What else? Er ... a camera, two pens, two watches ... oh, and a train ticket to Paris.

Track 1.30

1 a mobile phone
2 two business cards
3 an umbrella
4 a ticket

5 two keys
6 two buses
7 an orange
8 two passports
9 three watches

Track 1.31

eleven, twelve, thirteen, fourteen, fifteen, sixteen, seventeen, eighteen, nineteen, twenty, twenty-one, twenty-two, twenty-three, twenty-four, twenty-five, twenty-six, twenty-seven, twenty-eight, twenty-nine, thirty, forty, fifty, sixty, seventy, eighty, ninety, one/a hundred, one/a hundred and one

Track 1.32

1 sixty-six
2 twenty-three
3 seventy-nine
4 one hundred and one
5 eighty-eight
6 forty-five

Track 1.33

1 40   14
2 17   70
3 24   34
4 90   19
5 30   13
6 65   55

Track 1.34

How to say email addresses:
A: What's your email address?
B: It's jane.smith@email.com
at, dot, dot com, dash, underscore
jane dot smith at email dot com

Track 1.35

Judy: Come in. Sit down.
Anton: Thank you.
Judy: I'm Judy. What's your name?
Anton: My name's Anton Alekseev.
Judy: How do you spell *Alekseev*?
Anton: A–L–E–K–S–double E–V.
Judy: Where are you from, Anton?
Anton: I'm from Russia.
Judy: Oh, really? Where are you from in Russia?
Anton: I'm from Moscow.
Judy: Ah, Moscow is great. How old are you?
Anton: I'm twenty-six.
Judy: And are you married or single?
Anton: I'm single.
Judy: OK. What's your address here in Edinburgh?
Anton: It's 61 Leith Street. Leith is L–E–I–T–H.
Judy: What's the postcode?
Anton: It's EH3 6YI.
Judy: What's your phone number?
Anton: My mobile number is 07853 900841.
Judy: And last question: what's your email address?
Anton: It's anton.alekseev@my-mail.com.
Judy: OK, thank you very much!
Anton: You're welcome.

Unit 3

Track 1.36

bank, bus stop, café, car park, cashpoint, chemist, cinema, clothes shop, deli, park, petrol station, restaurant, shoe shop, station, supermarket

Track 1.37

1 a coffee
2 milk
3 a prawn salad
4 a cheese sandwich
5 sugar
6 an orange juice
7 a sparkling water
8 a tea
9 a piece of chocolate cake
10 a chicken roll

Track 1.38

1
A: Can I help you?
B: Yes. Can I have a piece of chocolate cake, please?
A: Eat in or take away?
B: Eat in, please.
A: Sure. Anything else?
B: Yes. A coffee, please.
A: With milk and sugar?
B: Milk, please. No sugar.

2
A: Hello. Can I help you?
B: Yes. Can I have a cheese sandwich, please?
A: Sure. Anything else?
B: Yes. Can I have a water too, please.
A: Still or sparkling?
B: Sparkling, please.

3
A: Good morning. Can I have a chicken roll and an orange juice, please?
B: Of course. Eat in?
A: No. Take away, please.
B: OK. Anything else?
A: No, thank you.

Track 1.39

/ɒ/ orange, chocolate, coffee, shop, doctor

Track 1.40

1 What's the restaurant's name?
2 It's not Jon's cheese roll.
3 Is the chocolate cake in the coffee shop good?

Track 1.41

A: Can I help you?
B: Yes. Can I have a piece of chocolate cake, please?
A: Eat in or take away?
B: Eat in, please.
A: Sure. Anything else?
B: Yes. A coffee, please.
A: With milk and sugar?
B: Milk, please. No sugar.

Audioscripts

Track 1.42
1 slow – fast
2 open – closed
3 hot – cold
4 expensive – cheap
5 bad – good
6 old – new
7 small – big

Track 1.43
/əʊ/ open, closed, slow, no, clothes

Track 1.44
1 Hello. Is your hotel open?
2 A: So, are you Joe?
  B: No, I'm Toby.
3 A: What's the hotel's number?
  B: It's 0900 485235.

Track 1.45
1
A: Hello. Is this shop open?
B: No, sorry. We're closed.
2
A: Can I have a coffee, please?
B: Big or small?
A: Small, please.
3
A: Wow! An Aston Martin. That's a really expensive car.
B: Yeah! $90,000. And it's very fast. 200 miles an hour!
4
A: Oh, hi! Er ... this is Liv. She's my new girlfriend.
B: Hi, Liv. I'm Emma. I'm Pete's old girlfriend.

Track 1.46
1
A: How much is the orange juice?
B: It's 89p.
2
A: How much is that computer?
B: It's $699.
3
A: How much is this sandwich?
B: It's €3.25.
4
A: How much is this mobile phone?
B: It's £75.
5
A: How much is that umbrella?
B: It's $6.99.
6
A: How much is this chocolate?
B: It's 10¢.

Track 1.47
1 €16.99
2 $90.00
3 £2.99
4 £17.99
5 £19.50
6 €1.15
7 €1.50
8 $19.00

Track 1.48
1
A: How much is this umbrella?
B: That blue umbrella is £6.50.
A: Oh, that's expensive.
B: Well, that green umbrella is only £4.99.
A: Hm ... It's very small. What's that?
B: It's an umbrella hat. Look, it's really good and it's only £5.50.
A: Er ... no, thank you. Can I have the blue umbrella, please?
B: Of course. That's £6.50, please.
A: Here you are.
B: Thank you. Here's your change.
A: Thank you.
2
A: What are those orange flowers?
B: They're called 'Birds of Paradise'.
A: They're beautiful. How much are they?
B: They're €10 each or €20 for three.
A: OK, can I have three, please.
B: Sure. Anything else?
A: Yes. How much are these chocolates?
B: They're €4.99.
A: OK. Can I have these, too, please? How much is that all together?
B: That's €24.99, please.
A: Can I pay by card?
B: Yes ... Enter your PIN number, please ... And here's your receipt.
A: Thank you.

Track 1.49
this flower, that umbrella, these chocolates, those flowers
A: What's this?
B: It's an umbrella hat.
A: What are those?
B: They're called 'Birds of Paradise'.

Track 1.50
black
blue
brown
green
grey
orange
pink
purple
red
white
yellow

Track 1.51
N = Nicklas, M = Magda
N: Hi, Magda.
M: Hello, Nicklas. How are you?
N: I'm fine, thanks. And you?
M: I'm OK, thanks. Where are you?
N: I'm in town, in Spring Park.
M: Oh, the park's nice at this time of year.
N: Yeah, it's really nice.
M: Is it hot?
N: Yes, it is. But my iced coffee is nice and cold.
M: That's good. How's your mum?
N: Oh, she's OK. She's on holiday.
M: Great! Where is she?
N: She's in Marrakesh, in Morocco.
M: Wow! Oh! I've got to go. See you on Friday evening?
N: Yes, see you on Friday.
M: Bye.
N: Bye.

Track 1.52
N: Hi, Magda.
M: Hello, Nicklas. How are you?
N: I'm fine,/I'm OK,/I'm not bad, thanks. And you?
M: Fine/OK/Not bad, thanks.

Unit 4

Track 1.53
airport, beach, gallery, lake, market, mountain, museum, national park, palace, river, the sea, theatre

Track 1.54
There is a palace.
There's a beautiful mosque.
There are some great museums.
There are two fantastic markets.
There are some fantastic shops.
There are a lot of good restaurants.

Track 1.55
1
Man 1: Excuse me. Is the National Theatre near here?
Dave: Yes, it is. We're right in front of it now.
Man 1: Oh! There it is. Thank you very much.
Dave: You're welcome. Bye.
2
Woman 1: Excuse me.
Dave: Yes. How can I help you?
Woman 1: Is there a café near here?
Dave: Yes, there is. There's one in the National Theatre.
Woman 1: Oh, great! Thank you.
Dave: You're welcome.
3
Man 2: Hello. Are there any car parks near here?
Dave: Yes, there are. There are two car parks on Stamford Street and there's another one on Belvedere Street, opposite Jubilee Gardens.
Man 2: Are they free?
Dave: No, they aren't. There aren't any free car parks in central London.
Man 2: OK. Thank you.
Dave: Bye.
4
Dave: Hello. Can I help you?
Woman 2: Are there any museums near here?
Dave: No, there aren't, I'm afraid. The big museums are in South Kensington.
Woman 2: Oh, alright. Thank you.
Dave: Bye.

5

Woman 3: Excuse me, is there a cashpoint near here?

Dave: Er ... no, there isn't. And there isn't a bank near here. The nearest cashpoint is on Waterloo Road I think. It's next to Waterloo East train station.

Woman 3: OK. Thanks for your help.

Dave: You're welcome. Bye.

Track 1.56

/θ/ think, three, thirty, theatre

/ð/ there, this, the, that, mother

Track 1.57

1 That's three pounds thirty, please. Thank you.

2 This is my brother and that's my father.

3 **A:** Are there any nice clothes in that shop?

   B: Yes, there are.

Track 1.58

Singular

There isn't a bank near here.

Is there a cashpoint near here?

Yes, there is./No, there isn't.

Plural

There aren't any free car parks.

Are there any museums near here?

Yes, there are./No, there aren't.

Any

Use **There aren't/Are there + any**

A: Are there any car parks near here?

B: No, there aren't.

There aren't any museums near here.

Track 1.59

A: Excuse me, is the National Theatre near here?

B: Yes, it is. It's just over there.

A: And are there any cafés near here?

B: Yes, there are. There's a café in the theatre.

A: OK. Thank you very much.

B: You're welcome.

Track 1.60

a

A: Excuse me. What time is it, please?

B: It's eleven o'clock.

b

A: Excuse me. What time is it?

B: It's half past six.

c

A: What's the time, please?

B: It's quarter past seven.

d

A: Excuse me. What's the time?

B: It's twenty-five past two.

e

A: What time is it, please?

B: It's quarter to six.

f

A: What time is it, please?

B: It's ten to twelve.

Track 1.61

Ten o'clock

Five past ten

Ten past ten

Quarter past ten

Twenty past ten

Twenty-five past ten

Half past ten

Twenty-five to eleven

Twenty to eleven

Quarter to eleven

Ten to eleven

Five to eleven

Track 1.62

1

A: Hello. Can I have a ticket to Glasgow Central, please?

B: Single or return?

A: Single, please.

B: That's £8.40, please.

A: Here you are. What time is the next train?

B: Let me see. It's at twenty past ten.

A: And what platform is it on?

B: It's on platform two.

A: Thanks very much.

2

A: Hello. Can I have a return to Gare de Lyon, please?

B: That's €10.90, please.

A: Can I pay by card?

B: Yes ... Enter your PIN number here. Thank you.

A: What time is the next train?

B: It's at ... quarter to two.

A: Oh! That's only five minutes.

B: It's platform six.

A: Thank you.

Track 1.63

A: Can I have a single to York, please?

B: That's £7.55 please.

A: Here you are. What time is the next train?

B: It's at four forty-five.

A: And what platform is it on?

B: It's on platform five.

Track 1.64

/ə/ seven, under, opposite, theatre, o'clock

Track 1.65

1 **A:** What's the time?

   B: It's eleven o'clock.

2 Is the theatre opposite the river?

3 Can I have a ticket to London?

Track 1.66

T = Teresa, N = Nikos, B = Barbara

T: Come with me, please. What are your names?

N: I'm Nikos and this is Barbara.

T: Nikos and Baba ...

B: Barbara! B–A–R–B–A–R–A.

T: Well, Nikos and Baba, I'm Teresa and ... this is your room.

N: Oh!

T: It's a very nice room. Here it is. There's a double bed and there's a shower.

N: Er ... are there any towels?

T: Yes, there are. There are some white towels on the bed, over there.

B: Is there an extra blanket?

T: Yes. There's a green blanket on the bed, next to the towels.

B: Great.

T: There's a kettle on the table with some tea and coffee ...

N: Is it fresh coffee?

T: No, it isn't, I'm afraid. It's instant coffee.

N: Oh!

B: Is there a fridge?

T: Yes, there is. It's under the table.

B: Is there a restaurant near here?

T: No, there isn't.

N: Or a café? Is there a café near here?

T: No, there isn't. There's a small shop about two miles from here.

N/B: Oh!

T: But it's closed today.

B: What time is breakfast?

T: It's from half past seven to half past ten.

N: And what time is checkout?

T: Checkout is quarter to twelve.

N/B: Oh.

B: Well ... er ... it's very nice.

N: Yes, ... beautiful.

T: Enjoy your stay!

N: Thanks. Bye. This room is awful!

B: I know – terrible!

Unit 5

Track 1.67

attractive, dark, fair, fat, old, overweight, short, slim, tall, thin, ugly, young

Track 1.68

AS = Annie Spring, AL = Aidan LeBlanc

AS: I'm Annie Spring and this is Vancouver Radio, Canada's favourite radio station. And now, on Vancouver Radio, it's time for ... 60-second interview. Today, my guest is Aidan LeBlanc! Welcome, Aidan.

AL: Thank you very much.

AS: Aidan is a writer. His first book is called *Short and Ugly*. It's a great title for a book!

AL: Thank you.

AS: And it's a great book!

AL: Oh, do you like it?

AS: Yes, I do. It's fantastic. Now, are you ready for your 60-second interview, Aidan?

AL: I'm ready.

AS: Here we go. Where are you from, Aidan?

AL: I'm from, Vancouver.

AS: Do you live in Vancouver now?

AL: Yes, I do. I live in a small house near the airport.

AS: Do you like Vancouver?

AL: Yes, I do. I like it a lot.

AS: Do you live alone?

AL: No, I don't. I live with my wife, Valeria.

AS: Valeria. That's a nice name. Is she Canadian?

AL: No, she isn't. She's from Venezuela.

AS: Do you have any children?

AL: Yes, I do. I have two daughters.

AS: How old are they?

AL: They're four and six and they're very beautiful. I'm short and ugly but they're beautiful.

AS: Ah, *Short and Ugly* is the title of your book. Do you like your job as a writer?

AL: Well ... I don't really work as a writer. It's my hobby. *Short and Ugly* is my first book.

AS: Oh, I see. So do you have another job?

AL: Yes, I do. I work for an international company.

AS: Do you work in an office?

AL: Yes, I do. I work in the accounts department.

AS: Do you like your job?

AL: No, not really!

AS: Really? That's a shame! So what do you like? What are your favourite things in life?

AL: Oh! I like fresh coffee, I like William Shakespeare, I like Puerto Cruz in Venezuela.

AS: And what are your least favourite things in life?

AL: Oh, I don't like airports. I think they're terrible. I don't like Hollywood films. I don't like ...

AS: Ah! Time is up. Thank you Aidan. Good luck with your new book – and your old job!

AL: Thank you.

AS: And now, some music.

Track 1.69

I like fresh coffee.

You have two daughters.

I live in a small house.

I don't work as a writer.

You don't like your job.

I don't live alone.

Do you have any children?

Yes, I do. / No, I don't.

Do you like your job?

Yes, I do. / No, I don't.

Track 1.70

/uː/ do, two, you, who, Vancouver

/əʊ/ don't, so, oh, euro

Track 1.71

1 **A:** That's two euros.
   B: I don't have two euros!

2 Where are you? Oh! Are you in the museum?

3 Do you like those new students from Vancouver?

Track 1.72

1 **A:** I like my job!
   B: Really? That's great!

2 **A:** I don't like my job.
   B: Really? That's a shame!

3 **A:** I don't work as a writer. It's my hobby.
   B: Oh, I see.

Track 1.73

He starts work early.

She finishes work late.

He doesn't watch TV.

She doesn't have a lot of time for me.

Does he have time?

Does he love coffee?

Yes, he does./No, he doesn't.

Track 1.74

/s/ works, gets, likes, eats

/z/ goes, lives, has, does

/ɪz/ finishes, watches

Track 1.75

1 'Does she work here?' 'Yes, she does.'

2 He likes food and he works in a restaurant.

3 She finishes work then she watches TV.

Track 1.76

Times of day

morning   afternoon   evening   night

Days of the week

weekdays: Monday Tuesday Wednesday Thursday Friday

the weekend: Saturday Sunday

Note:

in the morning/in the afternoon/in the evening

on Saturday/on Wednesday/on weekdays

at night/at the weekend

Track 1.77

call your friends

eat fish

make friends

play sport

say hello

stay at home

study a language

surf the Internet

Track 1.78

1 Where do you work?

2 What do you eat?

3 When do you get up?

4 How do you make friends?

5 Who do you work with?

Track 1.79

K = Katashi, V = Vera

K: Is the food nice?

V: Sorry?

K: The food. Is it nice?

V: Oh, yes, it is. The ham salad is great.

K: Oh. I don't eat meat.

V: Well, there's a cheese pizza, too.

K: My name's Katashi, by the way.

V: I'm Vera. Nice to meet you.

K: Nice to meet you, too. How do you know Paul?

V: We work together.

K: Really? What do you do?

V: I'm a doctor.

K: That's great. Where do you work?

V: I work at the hospital.

K: Oh, I see. Do you go to a lot of parties?

V: No, not really. At weekends I go to the gym or I go out with my friends. What about you? What do you do?

K: I'm a teacher.

V: Really? Where do you work?

K: In a language school in the centre of town.

V: I see. And what do you do at the weekend?

K: Oh, I stay at home and surf the Internet or I play sports. I really like squash.

V: I love squash, too. Where do you play?

Unit 6

Track 2.01

bathroom, bedroom, cellar, garage, garden, hall, kitchen, living room, loft, stairs

Track 2.02

Marisa

I live in a small flat near the centre of town. It's nice, but it's very expensive. There are two big bedrooms and the flat is about seventy square metres. The living room is big, but the kitchen is small.

Anya

I live in a small house. It's a nice house and it's near a park. There are three bedrooms and the house is about 120 square metres. The kitchen and the living room are small so we keep a lot of things in the loft.

Track 2.03

1 a table

2 a chair

3 an armchair

4 a bath

5 a toilet

6 a fridge

7 a coffee table

8 a lamp

9 a washing machine

10 a sink

11 a basin

12 a wardrobe

13 a mirror

14 a desk

15 a sofa

16 a bin

17 a cooker

18 a dishwasher

Track 2.04

1 iron your clothes

2 do the laundry

3 vacuum the stairs

4 sweep the floor

5 wash the dishes

6 tidy the living room

7 clean the bathroom

8 empty the dishwasher

9 lay the table

Track 2.05

1

A: Can you lay the table, please?

B: Yes, of course.

2

A: Can you tidy the living room, please?

B: No, I'm sorry. I can't. I'm very tired.

3

A: Can you clean the bathroom after your shower, please?

B: Sure, no problem.

4

A: Can you wash the dishes tonight, please?

B: No, I'm sorry. I can't. I'm really busy.

Track 2.06

/ʌ/ sometimes, does, mum, Monday

/ɪ/ dinner, dishes, living, bin

Track 2.07

1 What time does your mum make dinner?

2 I sometimes study Italian in the evening.

3 It's Sunday, so it's Mum's turn to wash the dishes.

Track 2.08

J = Jacob, A = Ahmad

J: Hi, Ahmad. Welcome!

A: Thanks, Jacob. Is anyone else here yet?

J: No, you're the first. Come in.

A: Thanks. Happy birthday! Here, this is for you.

J: Oh, thank you. That's really kind of you.

A: It's just something small. Hey, nice flat!

J: Thank you.

A: Wow! You've got a lot of books. Do you like reading?

J: Yes, I do. I love it. Do you?

A: Not really. I like surfing the Internet. You know, *Facebook*, *YouTube* ... . We've got wireless Internet in our flat, so I sometimes surf the Internet in bed!

J: Really? Would you like a drink?

A: Yes, please. I'd love one.

J: What would you like? I've got tea, coffee, apple juice ...

A: I'd like an apple juice, please. Is that your camera?

J: No, it's my flatmate's.

A: I really want to take good photos, but my photos are usually terrible.

J: Have you got a good camera?

A: No, I haven't. I want to buy a new camera, but I haven't got any money. I just use the camera on my mobile phone!

J: I think that's the problem!

A: Yeah! Nice TV. I love big flat-screen TVs.

J: It's my flatmate's. I don't like watching it. It's so big. In the evening I always want to read. I never want to watch TV.

A: Do you like watching films?

J: Sometimes. I like French films and Spanish films. What about you?

A: Yes, I do. I always watch big Hollywood films.

J: Really? I don't like watching Hollywood films. They're usually terrible. Now what's this present? Oh! It's a ... Hollywood film. Er ... thanks very much!

A: You're welcome!

Track 2.09

J: Would you like a drink?

A: Yes, please. I'd love one.

J: What would you like? I've got ...

A: I'd like an apple juice, please.

Track 2.10

1 Would you like a drink?

2 Would you like a hot drink or a cold drink?

3 Would you like an apple juice?

4 What would you like to eat?

Track 2.11

I like watching TV.

I want to buy a new phone.

I don't like surfing the Internet.

I don't want to take photos with my phone.

Do you like taking videos?

Do you want to listen to some music?

Track 2.12

A: Hello?

B: Hello. Does Helen live here? She's my friend.

A: I don't know. Can you describe Helen? Has she got a child?

B: No, she hasn't.

A: Does she like taking photos?

B: No, I don't think so.

A: Does she like playing computer games?

B: Yes, she does.

A: Has she got a big armchair and a lot of books?

B: Yes, she has.

A: Then I think Helen is in flat 4.

B: OK, great. Thank you.

A: You're welcome.

Unit 7

Track 2.13

1

I love cycling. So does Fran. We usually go at the weekend. Sometimes we go cycling in the park, but today we're here in the countryside. It's beautiful.

2

We meet every Sunday. We usually come here to the park and play chess. When the weather is bad we go to a café and do puzzles or just talk.

3

We always go for a walk in the park at the weekend. This park is beautiful and it's near our home. Our son always plays football and we just talk.

4

I usually do aerobics at the gym, but I've got this new game. It's a computer game and it's quite good fun.

Track 2.14

do aerobics   do puzzles   do exercise

go cycling   go for a walk   go to a gallery

play chess   play football   play tennis

Track 2.15

1

E = Eddie, J = Jo, G = Guard, W = Waiter

E: Here we are, Jo. A piece of chocolate cake for you and a cappuccino for me.

J: Thanks, Eddie. Mmm ... delicious! Chocolate cake isn't good for me, but I love it.

E: It's really cold in here.

J: Yes, it is.

E: So, what shall we do today?

J: Why don't we go to an art gallery? There's an exhibition at the modern art museum.

E: OK. That sounds nice. Let's go. I'm really cold.

J: Hold on. I've still got my chocolate cake. I hate eating fast!

2

E: Interesting paintings. What do you think of them?

J: I think they're ... awful.

E: Me too!

J: I don't like modern art.

E: The artist is Louise del Monte. Do you know her?

J: No, I don't. But I don't like her paintings. Shall we go to the cinema?

E: Yes, OK. But first I want to take a photo.

G: Excuse me. No photos in here. The signs are very clear. Please read them.

E: Oh, sorry.

J: Oh, my phone.

G: And no mobile phones.

J: Sorry!

E: Come on, let's go ... quick! I don't think he likes us!

3

E: What film do you want to see, Jo?

J: It's called *Wait and See*. It's a Jackie Chan film.

E: Jackie Chan?

J: Yeah. I really love him!

E: Let's have a look. That film starts at half past seven and it's only half past five now. That's two hours.

J: Oh, that's a long time. OK, why don't we see another film? There's a Julia Roberts film. Do you like her?

E: I don't mind her, but is there anything else?

J: Yes. There's a vampire film.

E: Oh, let's see that, Jo. I like watching vampire films.

J: I hate them. They're silly.

E: Maybe the cinema is a bad idea. Let's go and have dinner.

J: I'm not sure. I'm not very hungry.

E: There's a great restaurant near here.

J: Oh, OK. Let's go.

4

E: Hello. Table for two, please.

W: Have you got a reservation, Sir?

E: No, we haven't.

W: I'm afraid we're fully booked, Sir. I'm very sorry.

J: Oh no! It's not our day today.

Audioscripts

E: I've got an idea. Let's rent a DVD and watch it at your house. Then nothing can go wrong!

J: Good idea. Shall we get a takeaway pizza?

E: That sounds nice. I love watching films and eating pizza ...

5

E: Do you like the film, Jo?

J: I love it! How about you, Eddie?

E: Yeah. Clint Eastwood is brilliant. I love him.

J: I have an idea.

E: What?

J: Next time we want to have a day out, let's stay in!

E: Good idea!

Track 2.16

A: Shall we go to the cinema?

B: Yes, OK.

A: Why don't we go to an art gallery?

B: OK. That sounds nice.

A: Let's go and have dinner.

B: I'm not sure. I'm not very hungry.

Track 2.17

/aɪ/ like, mind, bike, cycling
/eɪ/ hate, play, eight, take

Track 2.18

1 I like taking photos and writing my blog.
2 I hate cycling in town at night.
3 I sometimes play tennis at eight in the morning.

Track 2.19

1 talk to animals
2 use a computer
3 dance
4 cook
5 write computer programs
6 speak French
7 play the piano
8 drive
9 sing

Track 2.20

1

Can people really talk to animals? Kevin Richardson can. Well, perhaps he can't talk to them, but he can understand them. Kevin lives and works in South Africa. He makes TV films about lions and other animals. He can look into their eyes and kiss them on the nose. How does he do it? 'Love and trust,' Kevin says.

2

Can you use a computer? Lim Ding Wen can and he can write computer programs. Ding Wen is nine years old and he lives in Malaysia. In his free time he writes programs for computers and mobile phones. What does Ding Wen's father say? 'It's easy. Everyone can do it.'

3

Olga and Inna Abelev are Russian twins in their 70s. They can speak over twenty

different languages. 'I sometimes talk to Olga in Chinese or Korean,' Inna says, 'and she talks to me in French or Italian.' The twins can't speak Japanese. 'I want to learn that next year,' Olga says.

Track 2.21

1 He can dance.
2 I can play the piano.
3 They can't sing.
4 You can't use a computer.

Track 2.22

1 I can speak English.
2 I can't speak Spanish.
3 She can't play the piano.
4 He can play the piano.
5 They can cook.
6 They can't do that.

Track 2.23

January, February, March, April, May, June, July, August, September, October, November, December

Track 2.24

W = Woman, M1 = Man 1, M2 = Man 2

1

W: Hello, TicketShop.

M1: Hello. I'd like to make a booking for *The High Life*.

W: When would you like to see the show?

M1: At the end of September. Have you got any tickets on Saturday the 29th of September?

W: I'm afraid that show is sold out in September. There are tickets in October.

M1: OK. Have you got any tickets on Saturday the 6th of October?

W: Yes, we have. How many tickets would you like?

M1: Two, please.

W: Would you like an afternoon or evening performance?

M1: Afternoon, please.

W: OK. Tickets are £42.50 each, so that's £85 altogether.

M1: OK. What time does the performance start?

W: Doors open at 7:00 and the performance starts at 7:45. Can I take your credit card number, please?

M1: Yes, it's 4308 32 ...

2

W: Good morning. TicketShop.

M2: Good morning. I'd like to make a booking for *The 51st State* concert.

W: OK. When would you like to see the show?

M2: On the 9th of June.

W: That's fine. How many tickets would you like?

M2: Four.

W: OK. Tickets are £21.50 each and there's a £2 booking fee. So that's £88 altogether.

M2: OK.

W: Doors open at 6:30 and the concert starts at 7:30. Would you like to pay by credit card or debit card?

M2: Credit card please.

W: OK. What's the credit card number?

Track 2.25

first, second, third, fourth, fifth, sixth, seventh, eighth, ninth, tenth, eleventh, twelfth, thirteenth, fourteenth, fifteenth, sixteenth, seventeenth, eighteenth, nineteenth, twentieth, twenty-first

Track 2.26

1 vegetables
2 potatoes
3 cheese
4 beef
5 chocolate
6 fish
7 seafood
8 fruit
9 rice
10 lamb
11 pasta
12 chicken

Track 2.27

W = Waiter, Wo = Woman, M = Man

W: Hello, Madam.

Wo: Hello. A table for two, please.

W: Certainly. Take a seat, please.

Wo: Thank you.

W: Would you like to order any drinks?

Wo: Yes. I'd like an orange juice, please.

M: I'd like a sparkling water, please.

W: Certainly.

...

W: Here are your drinks. Are you ready to order?

Wo: Er ... almost.

W: We've got some specials on the board over there.

M: Oh. Can you read them out for me?

W: Of course. For starters there's fish soup or there's chicken salad. And for the main course we have roast beef with roast potatoes and vegetables. Or we have a seafood pasta. Or there's lamb chops with rice.

Wo: Oh, I'd like the fish soup, please. And for the main course I'd like the roast beef.

W: And for you, Sir?

M: And I think I'd like the chicken salad, please.

W: Certainly. And for main course?

M: I think I'd like the seafood pasta.

W: Of course.

...

W: Can I take your plates?

Wo: Yes. Thank you.

W: Would you like a dessert? There's chocolate cake on the specials menu and we have fruit salad. Or we have cheese and biscuits.

Wo: Hmm, I don't really want a dessert. You?

M: No, not really. It's quite late. Let's go home and have coffee.

Wo: Good idea. Can we have the bill, please?

W: Yes, of course.

Track 2.28

A table for two, please.

Take a seat, please.

Would you like to order any drinks?

I'd like a sparkling water, please.

Are you ready to order?

For the main course I'd like the roast beef.

And for you, Sir?

I think I'd like the seafood pasta.

Can I take your plates?

Would you like a dessert?

Can we have bill, please?

Unit 8

Track 2.29

The first computer – 1946

The first moon landing – 1969

The first iPod – 2002

The first full-colour film – 1935

Track 2.30

H = Host, G = Gloria, K = Karen

H: And now it's time for *Famous Firsts*.

G: Great. I love this part of the show.

H: OK, Gloria. Try these: the first eBay auction?

G: Oh, that's interesting. Er … 2005?

H: No. 1995.

G: Oh, that's early. OK. Let's try another one.

H: The first photograph?

G: Oh, that's very old. Er … I don't know … 1896?

H: No, much earlier. 1826.

G: 1826? Really?

H: The first cashpoint?

G: Hmm … 1970?

H: Very close. 1971.

G: Oh, I'm not very good at this.

H: Let's talk to a caller. Who's on line one? Hello?

K: Hello.

H: What's your name?

K: I'm Karen.

H: OK, Karen. You know the rules. You just need one correct answer to win our top prize – a laptop computer. Are you ready?

K: I'm ready.

H: OK, number one. The first computer virus?

K: Oh, er, um, is it 1995?

H: No, it isn't. I'm sorry. It's 1981.

K: Oh, no.

H: Number two. The first horror film?

K: Oh, er … I don't know. 1940?

H: No, I'm sorry. It's 1896.

K: Oh dear.

H: Don't worry. You've got one more question. Here it is: the first Blu-ray film.

K: Er, um, is it 2006?

H: 2006?

K: Yes.

H: Karen … You are a winner!

Track 2.31

Number one is Grace Kelly. She was an actor.

Number two is Picasso. He was an artist.

Number three is Louis Armstrong. He was a musician.

Number four is Rudolf Nureyev. He was a dancer.

Number five is Florence Griffith Joyner. She was a sports star.

Number six is Agatha Christie. She was a writer.

Number seven is Andrew Carnegie. He was a business person.

Number eight is John F. Kennedy. He was a politician.

Number nine is Marie Curie. She was a scientist.

Number ten is Michael Jackson. He was a singer, a dancer and an actor.

Number eleven is Mahatma Gandhi. He was a writer, a leader and a politician.

Track 2.32

I was a student.

You were my best friend.

He was the eighth of ten children.

She was in *Rear Window*.

It was a great film.

You were Michael Jackson fans.

We were singers.

They were Michael's brothers.

Track 2.33

/ɜː/ were, person, thirty, first, her

Track 2.34

1 You were my first love.

2 My daughter is a beautiful girl. This is her photo.

3 They were my first friends. They're about thirty years old now.

Track 2.35

Who was on *Time* magazine's list of *The 100 Most Important People of the 20th Century*? Well, there were a lot of famous Americans like Michael Jackson, Marilyn Monroe and even Bart Simpson. But there were also people from other countries. The Japanese business person Akio Moriata was on the list. His company, Sony, makes electronic items and it is still famous today. And Coco Chanel was also on the list. She was a French fashion designer and business person. Her company, Chanel, makes perfume and clothes and is still very famous. And people like Francis Crick and James Watson were on the list. Crick and Watson were British scientists. They are famous for their work on DNA. They were Nobel Prize winners in 1962.

Track 2.36

D = Don, F = Fran, H = Helder

D: Your go, Fran.

F: Four! One, two, three, four.

D: Your first record or CD!

H: Thirty seconds. Starting NOW!

F: OK, I remember my first CD. It was about twenty years ago. It was *Macarena* by Los del Rio.

D: Was it a good song?

F: It was great! Hey, Macarena! It wasn't cool, but it was a fantastic song.

D: Los del Rio. Were they Spanish?

F: Yes, they were … . Oh no!

D: Bad luck, Fran. You can't say 'yes' or 'no'! It's your go now, Helder.

H: OK. Two. One, two. My first mobile phone.

F: Thirty seconds. Starting now!

H: OK, my first mobile phone was a Motorola.

F: Was it cheap?

H: Mobile phones weren't cheap then. This was in 1986.

D: Was it a small mobile phone like this one?

H: No, it wasn't … . Oh no!

F: Never mind, Helder. It's your go, Don.

D: One. Not again! My first holiday.

F: Thirty seconds. Starting now.

D: I remember my first holiday in another country. It was last year!

H: Really? Was it last year?

D: Yes! It was. Oh, no! I'm so bad at this game.

F: Don't worry, Don. It's only a game. My go again. Three! One, two, three. My first film at the cinema.

H: OK, thirty seconds, Fran. Starting now!

F: I remember my first film at the cinema. It was about twenty-five years ago and it was *Jaws 4*.

D: *Jaws 4*. Was it good?

F: It wasn't good. In fact, it was terrible. But I was so happy because I was at the cinema …

Track 2.37

1

Woman: How was your weekend?

Man: It wasn't very good. I was in bed all day on Saturday.

Woman: What was wrong with you?

Man: I don't know, but I'm OK now.

2

Girl 1: How was your date?

Girl 2: It was great. He was nice, and funny and he was really tall.

Girl 1: How tall was he?

Girl 2: Almost two metres, I think.

3

Neighbour: How was your holiday?

Mother: It was really nice. We were in Port Martin. There was no one on the beach, but it was quite far from the hotel.

Neighbour: How far was it?

Mother: About two kilometres.

4

Girl: Hi, Uncle Alan. How was your flight?

Uncle: It was OK, thanks, but it was quite long.

Girl: How long was it?

Uncle: About seven hours. And there weren't any free drinks!

Audioscripts

5
Son: Oh, hi. How was your trip?
Father: It was nice.
Son: There was ... er ... a party here.
Father: How big was the party?
Son: About fifty people. One or two are still here.

Track 2.38

/aʊ/ how, now, wow, house, mouse

Track 2.39

1 Wow! How big is that mouse?
2 Now, how far is the nearest town?
3 Do you want to have a shower at my house?

Unit 9

Track 2.40

Photo A – He sells fruit. He saves some money every month. He plays the lottery but he never wins any money.
Photo B – She invests in shares. She earns a lot of money.
Photo C – She spends a lot of money on clothes. She buys them online and pays by credit card.
Photo D – He borrows money from the bank. The bank lends him money.

Track 2.41

1 deliver newspapers
2 clean and tidy at home
3 work part-time in a cinema
4 wash cars
5 work nights in a factory
6 stack shelves
7 look after your neighbour's children
8 help your sister with her homework

Track 2.42

P = Presenter, R = Reporter, A = Amrik,
L = Lidia, E = Eva
P: ... and the weather tomorrow will be bright and sunny. Now, Sandy, what have you got for us?
R: Well, Paul. Did you know that some celebrities worked in very normal jobs before they were famous? For example, Nicole Kidman worked part-time in her local cinema and Tom Cruise delivered newspapers. So I asked some people around town, what was your worst job when you were a teenager?
R: What's your name?
A: My name's Amrik.
R: What do you do?
A: I'm a lawyer.
R: What was your worst job, Amrik, when you were a teenager?
A: Oh, let me see, well, when I was seventeen, I washed cars in a car wash at the weekend. It was awful.
R: Why was it awful?
A: Well, I started work at seven in the morning and I finished work at seven in the evening, so I was always tired. And

I just washed cars for twelve hours with only half an hour for lunch. My hands were red and sore every day. I hated it, but I stayed for two years.
R: What's your name?
L: I'm Lidia.
R: What do you do?
L: I'm a teacher.
R: What was your worst job when you were a teenager?
L: Oh, er ... well, when I was sixteen I worked nights in a supermarket in my holidays. It was awful.
R: Why was it awful?
L: Oh, I hated working in a supermarket. It was really hard work. I just stacked shelves. Oh, it was so boring.
R: What's your name and what do you do?
E: I'm Eva and I'm a university student.
R: What was your worst job, Eva, when you were a teenager?
E: My worst job? Well, I looked after my neighbours' children and they were really naughty, really bad. I didn't like that job. But it was different for my parents. My mum was seventeen when she arrived here. She worked nights in a factory. She hated it. It was really hard work and she earned almost nothing. She worked there for two years and then my dad started working in the same factory. After two years they started a restaurant. Now they've got five restaurants.
R: Five?
E: Yes. They cook in one of the restaurants together. They're workaholics – very different to me!

Track 2.43

/t/ liked, cooked, finished
/d/ cleaned, earned, lived
/ɪd/ hated, needed

Track 2.44

1 I listened to music.
2 They worked in a shop.
3 We watched TV.
4 She loved that job.
5 I texted him.

Track 2.45

1 rich
2 poor
3 careless with money
4 careful with money
5 generous
6 mean
7 broke

Track 2.46

/ɔː/ poor, four, more, sure, your
/iː/ mean, clean, three, she, street

Track 2.47

1 She's not poor, she's mean.
2 Is he forty-three or forty-four? I'm sure he's forty-four.

3 Shall we take a tour now? I want to see the city before we leave.

Track 2.48

750	seven hundred and fifty
999	nine hundred and ninety-nine
1,000	one thousand
2,500	two thousand five hundred
6,520	six thousand, five hundred and twenty
10,010	ten thousand and ten
300,502	three hundred thousand, five hundred and two
1,000,000	a/one million

Track 2.49

Today, football clubs buy and sell footballers for millions of pounds. But it wasn't always this way. In 1928 British club Arsenal spent £10,890 on David Jack. This was a world record. Thirty years later, in 1957, Juventus spent £93,000 on Omar Sivori, another world record. In 1973 Barcelona bought Johann Cryuff for £922,000. But the first million pound footballer was Guiseppe Savoldi. Napoli bought him for £1,200,000 in 1975. In the 1980s and 1990s prices went up fast. In 2000 Real Madrid spent £37 million on Luis Figo. Nine years later, in 2009, they spent £80 million on Cristiano Ronaldo.

Track 2.50

become	became
buy	bought
do	did
find	found
get	got
give	gave
go	went
have	had
sell	sold
spend	spent
take	took

Track 2.51

I = Interviewer, M = Imogen Moxley
I: So Imogen, tell me, you're a successful business woman and you're very careful with money. Were your parents careful with money?
M: Yes, they were. My father was a taxi driver and my mother was a housewife. They worked hard and they were careful with money. That was a good lesson for me.
I: Are you a saver or a spender?
M: I'm a saver. Before I was twenty-five I spent my money on holidays and shopping. Then I married Gary and in 2011 I had my first child. Now I save my money.
I: How do you usually pay for things: cash, card or cheque?
M: I always pay by card. I only have one card because I only need one card. I don't usually have money in my bag.
I: Do you always give big tips?
M: Yes, I do. My father was a taxi driver, so I always give taxi drivers big tips. I also give waiters tips.

I: What financial advice do you give to young people?

M: Work hard. That's really important. And don't buy a big house in a bad area. Buy a small house in a good area!

I: Thank you very much, Imogen.

M: You're welcome.

Unit 10

Track 2.52

Love and family: fall in love, get married, have a baby, meet someone special
House: leave home, move
Personal: get fit, learn to drive
School/University: go to university, graduate
Work: change jobs, get a job, quit your job, retire, start your own business

Track 2.53

Woman
About five years ago I quit my job. I was bored and I wanted to study. I went to university and I studied maths. I graduated last year. Now I'm a maths teacher in a school. My job isn't easy, but I really love it.

Man
When I was eighteen, I left home. I found a house with a friend and we lived there for five years. Then I met someone special – Belinda. We fell in love and got married. That was three years ago. And guess what! Last year we had a baby.

Track 2.54

I'm going to go with them.
You're going to wait for me.
He's going to lend me some money.
You're going to visit me next year.
We're going to see Ayers Rock.
They're going to drive to Wellington tomorrow.

Track 2.55

1 We're really happy.
2 I'm so excited.
3 I'm bored.
4 I'm scared.
5 I'm so angry.
6 I'm really nervous.
7 I'm upset.
8 I'm depressed.
9 I'm tired.

Track 2.56

Dialogue a
S = Seth, P = Pippa

S: Oh, hi, Pippa. What's the matter? Are you OK?

P: Not really, Seth. I lost my phone yesterday, so I borrowed my husband's phone. Now I can't find it.

S: Oh no! What are you going to do?

P: I don't know yet.

S: Are you going to tell him?

P: Yes, of course I am. I'm not going to lie to him.

S: Is he going to be angry?

P: He isn't going to be happy!

S: Are you going to buy him a new one?

P: I really don't know, Seth.

S: Oh, OK.

P: Sorry. I didn't mean to be angry with you.

S: That's OK. I'm late. See you soon.

P: See you soon, Seth. Bye.

S: Yeah, bye.

Dialogue b
K = Kerry, O = Omar

K: See you on Monday, Omar.

O: Yeah, see you on Monday, Kerry.

K: Is everything OK, Omar?

O: Oh, yes and no. My children are going to leave home soon.

K: Oh? How old are they?

O: Ravi is twenty-two and Sef is nineteen.

K: Where are they going to go?

O: Ravi is going to live with his friend and Sef is going to go to university.

K: That's great!

O: Yes, but they aren't going live at home with me and my wife any more. We're going to miss them.

K: Cheer up, Omar. They aren't going to live in another country.

O: Yes, that's true. Thanks, Kerry.

K: Have a nice weekend!

O: You too. Bye.

Track 2.57

1
Seth: I'm late. See you soon.
Pippa: See you soon, Seth. Bye.

2
Kerry: See you on Monday, Omar.
Omar: Yeah, see you on Monday, Kerry.

3
Kerry: Have a nice weekend!
Omar: You too. Bye.

Track 2.58

I'm not going to borrow his phone again.
He isn't going to like me.
They aren't going to live at home.
Are you going to buy him a new one?
Yes, I am./No, I'm not.
Is he going to be happy?
Yes, he is./No, he isn't.
Are they going to go to university?
Yes, they are./No, they aren't.
What are you going to do?
Where are they going to go?

Track 2.59

1
A: They're tired.
B: Are they going to go to bed early?
A: Yes, they are.

2
A: I'm bored.
B: Are you going to watch TV?
A: No, I'm not.

3
A: She's angry.
B: Is she going to talk to him?
A: Yes, she is.

4
A: He's depressed.
B: Is he going to go to the doctor?
A: No, he isn't.

5
A: I'm excited.
B: Are you going to tell your parents?
A: Yes, I am.

6
A: They're scared.
B: Are they going to call the police?
A: No, they aren't.

Track 2.60

Why did you buy a DVD?
I bought a DVD because it's Adam's birthday.
Why did you quit your job?
Because I hated it and because I want to live abroad.

Track 2.61

1 Why do you go to the gym?
2 Why do you like your job?
3 I bought him a book because he wants to learn to read.
4 I went to the doctor because I needed some medicine.

Track 2.62

1 a toy
2 a photo frame
3 chocolates
4 beauty products
5 tickets for a show
6 a clock
7 a vase
8 jewellery
9 a plant
10 plates and bowls
11 glasses
12 a voucher for a shop

Track 2.63

A: This is for you.
B: Oh, thank you. That's really kind of you.
A: Don't mention it./You're welcome.

Pronunciation bank

Track 2.64

1 /ɪ/, big, /æ/, bag. It's a big bag.
2 /ɪ/, sit, /i:/, seat. Can I sit in this seat?
3 /æ/, map, /ɒ/, mop. That's my map and my mop.
4 /ɪ/, live, /ʌ/, love. I love living in London.
5 /ʌ/, cup, /æ/, cap. The cup is under your cap.
6 /i:/, me, /ɔ:/, more. Please give me more.
7 /ɪ/, ship, /ɒ/, shop. There's a shop on the ship.
8 /ɪ/, lift, /e/, left. The lift is on the left.
9 /ɑ:/, car, /i:/, key. Where's my car key?
10 /ɒ/, box, /ʊ/, books. Look at the box of books.
11 /i:/, he, /ɜ:/, her. He hates her.
12 /i:/, Sophie, /ə/, sofa. Sophie's on the sofa.
13 /e/, let, /eɪ/, late. Let's get up late.

14 /aɪ/, kite, /eɪ/, Kate. This is Kate's kite.

15 /iː/, she, /əʊ/, show. She's at the show.

16 /iː/, eat, /eɪ/, eight. Did Jane eat eight cakes?

17 /aʊ/, how, /aɪ/, Hi. Hi. How are you?

18 /iː/, week, /eɪ/, wake. I wake up at six in the week.

19 /p/, Paul, /b/, ball. Put Paul's ball in the bin.

20 /t/, to, /d/, do. What do you want to do?

21 /k/, came, /g/, game. He came and played a game.

22 /tʃ/, chess, /dʒ/, Jess. Jess plays chess.

23 /f/, off, /v/, of. Please get off of Fran's van.

24 /p/, pink, /θ/, think. I think it's pink.

25 /p/, pay, /ð/, they. Did they pay for the party?

26 /s/, keeps, /z/, keys. She keeps her keys in her bag.

27 /t/, fit, /ʃ/, fish. Is your fish fit?

28 /t/, letter, /ʒ/, leisure. This letter's about leisure.

29 /m/, mice, /n/, nice. Are your mice nice?

30 /l/, collect, /r/, correct. Did you collect the correct letter?

Track 2.65

One syllable words
one, six, big, young, read, learn, friend, great, lake, house, beach, road, west

Two syllable words: stress on first syllable
happy, seven, listen, morning, passport, father, website, surname, photo, awful, teacher, picture, modern, Sunday

Two syllable words: stress on second syllable
Japan, address, between, today, return, behind, Chinese, design, July, explain, mistake, dessert, because

Three syllable words: stress on first syllable
India, favourite, gallery, holiday, beautiful, Saturday, visitor, newsagent, medium, popular, opposite, interview, architect, hospital

Three syllable words: stress on second syllable
eleven, computer, cathedral, espresso, attachment, important, piano, designer, reporter, together, September, tomorrow, exciting, potato

Three syllable words: stress on third syllable
afternoon, engineer, introduce, magazine